MW00936916

CHRIST

THE TRANSFORMING POWER OF GOD'S LOVE AND GRACE

IN ME

Paul Nordman

xulon PRESS

Copyright © 2016 by Paul Nordman

Christ in Me
The Transforming Power of God's Love and Grace
by Paul Nordman

Printed in the United States of America.
Edited by Xulon Press.

ISBN 9781498480642

All rights reserved solely by the author. The author guarantees all contents are original and do not infringe upon the legal rights of any other person or work. No part of this book may be reproduced in any form without the permission of the author. The views expressed in this book are not necessarily those of the publisher.

Unless otherwise indicated: Scripture taken from the HOLY BIBLE, NEW INTERNATIONAL VERSION. Copyright © 1973, 1978, 1984 International Bible Society. Used by permission of Zondervan Bible Publishers. All rights reserved.

Scripture quotations marked (ESV) are from The Holy Bible, English Standard Version® (ESV®), copyright © 2001 by Crossway Bibles, a publishing ministry of Good News Publishers. Used by permission. All rights reserved.

When noted as (NASB), Scripture taken from the NEW AMERICAN STANDARD BIBLE®, Copyright © 1960, 1962, 1963, 1968, 1971, 1972, 1973, 1975, 1977, 1995 by The Lockman Foundation. Used by permission.

When noted as (The Message), Scripture taken from THE MESSAGE. Copyright © 1993, 1994, 1995, 1996, 2000, 2001, 2002. Used by permission of NavPress Publishing Group.

Confession of Freedom. Copyright © 2014 Paul Edward Nordman. Used by permission. All rights reserved.

www.xulonpress.com

Praise for *Christ in Me*

Paul Nordman has keen insight into the life of faith. He keeps one eye on the Cross, where Jesus finished his work, once and for all, and the other on the Spirit, who continues his work in each and every one who believes. Paul opened my eyes to my new identity "in Christ," and how Christ's Spirit is working out that new identity "in me." With a fine ear for a turn of phrase and an apt analogy, Paul in 174 short pages illuminates what I've been trying to preach for fourteen years. Highly recommended!

—Eric Waters
Senior Pastor, St. John Lutheran Church, Boerne, Texas

Christ in Me points us to a mature walk in Christ and shows how He truly does set us free. Paul's book inspired me, and I highly recommend it to all.

—Steve Johnston
CEO, Cincinnati Insurance Companies

Paul Nordman's daily reflections draw us back to the place of first importance—our need to depend fully on Christ. The world and our flesh pull us away to self-sufficiency, but these daily readings will help draw you back to the truth of God's incredible love and grace.

—Melissa Spoelstra

Bible teacher and author of *First Corinthians, Living Love When We Disagree* and *Total Family Makeover: 8 Practical Steps to Making Disciples at Home*

Through real-life stories and helpful analogies, Paul's book captures the heart and instills in it the desire to apply God's word to everyday struggles and opportunities. Never have I been so encouraged and called to action through a devotional book.

—Cindy Monroe

Founder & CEO, Thirty-One Gifts

It is easy to fall into the trap of trying to live the Christian life in our own power, through a facade of self-sufficiency. Through page after page of relatable stories and observations, *Christ in Me* reminds us that not only is this impossible, it is also far inferior to walking through this life with God, enjoying His presence and love each step of the way. God is magnified in this book, and I recommend it wholeheartedly.

—Matthew Nordman

Author's favorite (only) son

It is no easy task to illuminate "meat truths" of Scripture in a manner that both informs the mind and strengthens the heart. Yet, to follow the apostle Paul's command to "*be strong in the grace that is in Christ Jesus*" it is essential that both are fully engaged as we sit alone with the Lord. In this devotional, Paul Nordman stewards his gifting with a unique blend of creativity, depth of insight on the riches of grace, and humility that caused this reader to look within, and then upward.

—Doug Patch
Pastor, Xenos Christian Fellowship, Columbus, Ohio

Table of Contents

A Helpful Introduction

I t was during the Christmas holidays when I took some "prayer walks" over a several-day period. My wife, Peggy, had introduced the concept when we were dating, and I've been grateful for it ever since. Talking while walking, my conversation with God is always longer, deeper, and more open and refreshing. I speak and God listens; He speaks and I am at peace. We are friends. On our first stroll together, I found myself confessing to God some specific sin patterns in my life: pride and fear, among others. There was no harshness, no beating myself up, and no cowering before Him. Rather, this was a refreshing time of open and honest response to His Holy Spirit, for He had gently revealed these shortfalls to a heart that had come to trust Him. I'd long ago learned to discern between the devil's sharp, accusatory tones—always meant to berate, harm, discourage, and destroy—and the Spirit's gentle, caring voice of correction and guidance. This was the latter, so I was eager to listen, understand, and respond.

"Lord, I tend to harbor fear," I began, "It is part of my sinful nature, a weakness in my soul. I don't like this pattern, and I know you don't like it, either. Yet, you care for me and want only the best for me. I am very sorry for allowing myself to succumb to fear."

There is something uplifting in coming to terms with the reality of our wrongs. Revealing our sins, the Spirit is a trusted counselor who helps us see events and thoughts that weigh us down and prevent us from living life better. Great is our relief, then, as we align ourselves with God's truth and will in a matter. Assured of His forgiveness, we breathe easier. We are at peace with Him.

As we continued our prayer walk, I marveled at the fact that Jesus had given in to none of the temptations that had ensnared me. While I am naturally inclined to be prideful, Jesus lives in humility. When it comes to spiritual things, I am weak, but the Son of God knows only strength. Impure doesn't even begin to describe my sin-stained soul, but the Redeemer exudes holiness. No, Jesus could not be rightly accused of any wrongdoing; no sin could describe Him.

Trekking on, I mused over what Jesus had said about Him living in me, like a vine to a branch He said, and me living in Him like a branch from a vine. The vine is not the branch, nor vice versa, but they live united as one. Likewise, it is the will of God—His design—that we live as one with Him and in Him. In fact, Jesus petitioned His Father that this be so. Hadn't the apostle Paul, also, spoken of the now-revealed mystery of Christ living in us? To him, Jesus was more than religion and faith in Christ more than relationship. Paul proclaimed Christ in him to be transformational, a matter of new identity: "I no longer live," he wrote, "but Christ lives in me."[1]

It occurred to me that, if Jesus lives in me—if He has grafted this branch into Himself, the vine—then His character qualities flow through me, nourishing me in new life—His life. His peace becomes my peace, His strength builds me up, and I am humbled before His humility for this is His nature and His desire for me. Moreover, God does not merely deem us from afar to be righteous and holy and redeemed; rather, Christ has actually *"become for us* wisdom from God—that is, our righteousness, holiness and redemption."[2] So our walk that began in confession of sin now ended in celebration of all God has done in and for His people and in joy over the freedom and life we find in Him.

We began our second prayer walk together. As one leafless tree after another passed by my periphery that winter day, I warmly recalled our earlier conversation. The pattern was clear and consistent: my natural inclinations are always different than God's. Jesus, however, lived this earthly life perfectly pleasing to God; and, because He now lives in me, His divine nature—His character—lives also in me. Mine is but to give myself over to Him and His transformative work.

---

[1] Galatians 2:20
[2] 1 Corinthians 1:30

What emerged, then, was a confession of who Christ is and, therefore, who He is in all who live in Him:

By nature, I am anxious, but there is no anxiousness in Christ.
Christ is my life, and Christ in me is peace.

By nature, I transgress, but there is no transgression in Christ.
Christ is my life, and Christ in me is redemption.

By nature, I am captive, but there is no captivity in Christ.
Christ is my life, and Christ in me is freedom.

By nature, I am fearful, but there is no fear in Christ.
Christ is my life, and Christ in me is confidence.

By nature, I am condemned, but there is no condemnation in Christ.
Christ is my life, and Christ in me is salvation.

By nature, I am sinful, but there is no sin in Christ.
Christ is my life, and Christ in me is righteousness.

By nature, I am weak, but there is no weakness in Christ.
Christ is my life, and Christ in me is strength.

By nature, I am impure, but there is no impurity in Christ.
Christ is my life, and Christ in me is holiness.

By nature, I am foolish, but there is no foolishness in Christ. Christ is my life, and Christ in me is wisdom.

By nature, I am prideful, but there is no pridefulness in Christ. Christ is my life, and Christ in me is humility.

By nature, I am despairing, but there is no despair in Christ. Christ is my life, and Christ in me is hope.

By nature, I am dying, but there is no death in Christ. Christ is my life. Forever.

How amazing God's will is for us! How refreshing His presence is in us! How great is His love! Most of us who have placed our faith in Christ would agree we have experienced the peace of His presence, the relief of our redemption, and a thankfulness for His faithfulness. We have known the freedom of forgiveness and the delight of discovering Him to be true. Our heart is gladdened by salvation, our life has meaning, and we are humbled in God's love. Looking inward, we see changes only his Spirit could have brought about in us.

Yet so many of us would also confess a dissonance in our experience, a disharmony between the faith we gratefully profess and the way we so often act or feel in our day-to-day lives. Why is it, for instance, our mouths sing praises in church on Sunday, yet sling curses at work on Monday? How do we drink in helpful devotionals over Tuesday morning coffee, only to spew out hurtful criticisms over Wednesday afternoon tea? Did I really plead mercy for me on Thursday and then withhold it from my family on Friday? By Saturday night, we feel nothing like we did last Sunday morning. And we ask, "What happened?"

Living in Conflict

Our struggles in the world around us make more sense when we recognize the spiritual battle within us. We all carry around what the apostle Paul called our "sinful nature,"[3] or "old self."[4] The sin nature is that self-willed part of us that wants to live life on our own terms and not God's. Its "me first" filter influences our thought processes, our word choices, and our actions, sometimes even in subtle ways, as when we do good deeds for our own sense of moral accomplishment.

Yet for all who trust in Christ, the apostle Peter proclaims participation in a new nature, a "divine nature."[5] In the same way, Paul points to a "new self."[6] For in the gospel, writes Paul, God has revealed His long-held mystery: "Christ in you, the hope of glory."[7] It was God's plan—His deep desire—not only to live with us in restored relationship, but for His Spirit to dwell in us as our new identity. Certainly we are not God;

[3] Romans 7:18
[4] Ephesians 4:22
[5] 2 Peter 1:4
[6] Ephesians 4:24
[7] Colossians 1:27

rather, when Christ moves in, He brings all of the characteristics found in Him and He shares these with us.

Should we be surprised, then, when Paul enlightens us to the unseen goings-on within us, a "tension between the traits," so to speak? "The sinful nature desires what is contrary to the Spirit," he wrote, "and the Spirit what is contrary to the sinful nature. They are in conflict with each other . . ."[8] The sinful nature of our old self would tether us to a self-centered existence, even as the divine nature of the Spirit would shine forth from us in love for God and for our fellow sojourners in this life. No wonder our spiritual Sunday devolved into a troubled Tuesday and further into a frustrating Friday! "What happened," we ask? It was nothing short of an other-worldly clash with us at ground-zero.

Thriving in Grace

We are saved by grace through faith in Christ Jesus. We know this, we thank God for this, and we breathe a deep sigh of relief, for no amount of our own power or effort could spare us from the consequences of our sin. Our salvation truly is a gift from God. So, too, is our sanctification: our character is transformed to be like Christ, not by self-willed assertions of a righteousness we do not possess but through the work of the Spirit of God who imputes to us the righteousness of

---

[8] Galatians 5:17

Christ. Spiritual birth and spiritual growth—both are gifts of a loving God eager to bless a grateful us who look to Him in faith. For the Spirit is as certain to mold us into the image of Christ as He was to give us life in His name. He transforms us from the inside out.

Reading This Book

Christ in Me is written as a series of reflections that look at life as people in whom Christ lives by faith. For each of the confessions on pages xvi and xvii, this book offers four daily readings that recognize our inclination to insist on our way and not God's, yet celebrate the presence of Christ who lives in us to lead us in His higher, fuller, and freer ways. Though temptations still tantalize our old self, by the Spirit's power we trust the Spirit's lead and follow him in God's paths and for His good pleasure. When we do fail and give into sin, however, we do not run away from God in fear and doubt, compounding our wrong; instead, we turn from our wandering ways, run to God, and offer ourselves again to His Spirit in us, humbled in His love and thankful for His grace. And lifting our gaze beyond ourselves, we reach out and share Christ with a world still searching for grace, even as we serve them in His name.

Before beginning your devotional time in this book, pause for a moment and ask God to send His Holy Spirit to help you redirect your thoughts away from the busyness of the day and onto Him. Open your heart to the Spirit's care as you read, accepting His love for you and trusting Him to transform you into the likeness of Christ. Then respond to God in prayer, believing His promises, offering yourself to His guidance, and thanking Him for His faithfulness each day.

To Peggy,
It is an honor to journey through life with you.

Acknowledgments

To my family, thank you for your love and friendship. God has blessed us.

To Chuck Coleman, Dave Mann, John Ness, Eric Nordman, Matthew Nordman, Peggy Nordman, Eric Waters, and Lisa Zager, thank you for reviewing early excerpts or drafts and for offering your helpful insights. This is a better book because of you.

To Judy Webb, thank you for inviting me to contribute to the church blog. Who knew it would lead to this?

To many encouragers along the way, you have no idea the impact of your kind words of support. You have not only kept me writing, you have shown me the beauty of the body of Christ. Thank you.

1

Christ in Me Is Peace

By nature, I am anxious,
but there is no anxiousness in Christ.
Christ is my life, and Christ in me is peace.

Finding Peace with God

Grace and peace to you from God our Father.
(Colossians 1:2)

I knew a man who graduated from seminary and became a pastor yet did not know Jesus Christ. One day as he was preparing his sermon, the Scripture text resounded from its pages, speaking life and truth into the deepest chambers of this man's soul. Alone in his study, he shouted his discovery out loud, "Jesus, you're real!" Over his remaining years, he was filled with joy, the elation that accompanies peace with God, and he spoke unabashedly of his love for Jesus.

Despite our contrasting views of who God is and what He is like, most people relate to the expression, "finding peace with God." Now if we can identify with the quest to find such peace—or the jubilation of having done so—then the sense of separation from God must also be an experience common to humanity, for our shared pursuit of peace with God exposes the discord that exists between us in the first place.

Our ways are not His ways, and we know it. Our will conflicts with His will, and there is friction. Our

The peace we desire enough to pursue, God desired enough to provide.

best falls short of His good, and we lack peace. "If only you had paid attention to my commands, your peace would have been like a river, your righteousness like the waves of the sea,"[1] said God to His people through the prophet Isaiah. Instead, we are disquieted. Like the psalmist, we are "troubled by [our] sin."[2] As well we should be! Sin is problematic; it exists as a schism between a sullied people and a holy God.

Yet in His holiness, our God is also a loving God. Do we think we want peace with Him? He wants it even more. Are we troubled by the separation between us? It bothers Him even more, not as One who needs us, but as One who loves us; not as One who is helpless to unite us, but as the only One who can bring us peace. And so He has. In fact, it pleased Him to do so! Peering over the shoulder of the Colossian church, we read their mail from the apostle Paul: "For God was pleased to have all his fullness dwell in [Jesus], and through him to reconcile to himself all things, whether things on earth or things in heaven, by making peace through his blood, shed on the cross."[3]

Then how do we experience it? By entrusting ourselves entirely to Jesus who reconciled us to God. The Bible calls it faith. "Therefore, since we have been justified through faith, we have peace with God through our Lord Jesus Christ, through whom we have gained access by faith into his grace

---

[1] Isaiah 48:18
[2] Psalm 38:18
[3] Colossians 1:19, 20

in which we now stand."[4] The peace we desire enough to pursue, God desired enough to provide. Christ won our peace. Christ *is* our peace. We can trust Him with our lives and have peace.

"Jesus, you're real!" Amen, brother.

Your faith has saved you; go in peace. (Luke 7:50)

---

[4] Romans 5:1, 2

Don't Worry, Be Practical

Peace I leave with you; my peace I give you. I do not give to you as the world gives. Do not let your hearts be troubled and do not be afraid.
(John 14:27)

If I could go back and change one thing in my life, it would be this: I would not have worried so much. For all the energy I've invested in it, worry has yielded nothing in return. At best, it has been a terrible distraction, and more often, an obstacle that's only made matters worse. Jesus said we would have troubles in this world, but He encouraged us—even commanded us—to choose not to worry about them. Worry comes naturally to us who want to control our future yet cannot, and it doubts the God who knows our tomorrows and rules over them in sovereignty! So with renewed minds, let's look "worry" squarely in the eye and expose this heartless foe for what it is.

Worry is tantamount to adding *potential* problems of the *future* to our list of *actual* problems of the *present*. Jesus told us, for instance, not to worry about what we *will* eat . . . or what we *will* drink . . . or what we *will* wear.[5] Instead, He assured us that our heavenly Father knows what we need and will give us what we need, just as He always has.[6] *We can rest in such comfort.*

---

[5] Matthew 6:25
[6] Matthew 6:32, 33

When it comes down to it, worrying is just not practical. "Who of you by worrying can add a single hour to his life?"[7] Jesus asked. When we are striving to meet a deadline, for instance, does our worry advance us toward our objective, or does it divert our attention from the pressing task at hand? Isn't it true that worry can paralyze us into indecision or rush us into poor decisions? It is far better to trust God and apply ourselves free of distraction. *We can thrive in such confidence.*

A manager once told me, "The dread of anticipation is worse than the pain of reality." Haven't we found things almost never materialize exactly as we fear they will? Perhaps that's why Jesus said, "Do not worry about tomorrow, for tomorrow will worry about itself. Each day has enough trouble of its own."[8] This is not to say we shouldn't *plan* for tomorrow — we should — but we shouldn't *worry* about tomorrow. *We can flourish in such wisdom.*

Jesus warned us that worries and other distractions in life "choke the word, making it unfruitful."[9] They tempt us first to distrust God and then to disobey Him. But when we submit ourselves to God's rule in our lives, we find Him true to His word and faithful to His people. "Grace, peace and mercy from God the Father and from Jesus Christ, the Father's Son, will be with us in truth and love."[10] *We can rejoice in such peace.*

---

[7] Matthew 6:27
[8] Matthew 6:34
[9] Mark 4:19
[10] 2 John 3

I have told you these things, so that in me you may have peace. In this world you will have trouble. But take heart! I have overcome the world. (John 16:33)

Cash for Clunkers

> *Do not be anxious about anything, but in every-*
> *thing, by prayer and petition, with thanks-*
> *giving, present your requests to God. And the*
> *peace of God, which transcends all under-*
> *standing, will guard your hearts and your*
> *minds in Christ Jesus. (Philippians 4:6, 7)*

So let me get this straight. You're telling me I can hand my anxieties over to God, and He will give me His peace in return? Are you serious? This is like "cash for clunkers," only better! Where do I sign?

There is nothing God doesn't know about us. He knows our fear over the threats we face today; He knows our worries about what may (or may not) happen tomorrow. God knows the anxieties that churn within us, and He knows they only add to the troubles that spawned them. In fact, He cares so much that He has already responded with a solution to our fears: a command for us to obey and a promise for Him to keep.

Our charge is to trade in our clunkers. "Cast all your anxiety on him because he cares for you,"[11] encouraged Peter. This does not come naturally to us; we would rather hoard anxiety like scrap metal in a junkyard of jitters. It is our dis-

---

[11] 1 Peter 5:7

belief and self-will, rather, that beget anxieties in the first place; then they accumulate into a heap too heavy for us to handle. Instead, we are called to do the unnatural—to adjust our thinking, trust God, and relinquish to Him our stress.

So we start by choosing to believe God's promises instead of our doubts. Then we act on His command to trust, talking with God, humbly asking Him for guidance through the troubles before us, and—very importantly—expressing our gratitude to Him for hearing and granting our request. What does God promise in return? Gold. When we step forward in belief, He takes our anxious wrecks and gives us in exchange a peace far greater than our ability to comprehend. Our circumstances may change, but even if they don't, He will walk us right through them in an otherwise unknowable peace. Be it through a Scripture that "leaps off the page," the care of others, astounding events that transpire before us, or that quiet but unmistakable assurance within, we will know His presence. For our peace is a person: Jesus Christ, the Son of God.

My anxiousness for God's peace? I'll take that trade any day!

> *You keep him in perfect peace whose mind*
> *is stayed on you, because he trusts in you.*
> *(Isaiah 26:3 ESV)*

Making Peace

When you enter a house, first say, "Peace to this house." (Luke 10:5)

D on't you love those "small world" moments when in conversation with someone, you discover you both know the same person? There's the brief moment of surprise, usually followed by smiles and perhaps even laughter as you fondly reflect on the uniqueness of the one you know in common.

Through the years, I've noticed the same thing among those of us who, in faith, have come to know Jesus Christ— our hearts are warmed when we find another who is also friends with Him. No matter how different our backgrounds, our personalities, or our journeys to the cross, we all discover the same Christ and receive His same Spirit within us. Not only are we delighted at knowing this One in common, we experience His peace, share in His joy, and celebrate the inner freedom we find in Him.

So if this Christ brings such goodness to us, and if He's brought the same to our mutual acquaintances, why not introduce Him around a bit? "Blessed are the peacemakers," Jesus said, "for they will be called sons of God."[12] He didn't have in mind mere detente or the suppression of conflict among

[12] Matthew 5:9

self-willed people. As welcome as even that modicum of relief can be, peace with God is much more than that—a deep wellbeing of the spirit, mind, and soul that comes from being reconciled with Him. Nor was Jesus suggesting we compromise truth in order to be on good terms with others. On the contrary, He is truth, and it is He himself who brings deep satisfaction and restored relationship with God.

We sometimes mistake sharing our faith as a match of wits played across the table from an opponent. But isn't it really standing alongside of people just like us and introducing them to Jesus, knowing He will bring peace to them, just as He has to us? What higher calling could there be? What better gift could we give than the shared smiles, laughter, and fondness for the One we will know in common forever? He won't disappoint.

Peacemakers who sow in peace raise a harvest of righteousness. (James 3:18)

2

Christ in Me Is Redemption

By nature, I transgress,
but there is no transgression in Christ.
Christ is my life, and Christ in me is redemption.

What We All Share in Common

The Bible study at the drop-in center for trafficked women had just concluded for the day when one of the participants approached the Salvation Army social worker on behalf of the group. "You always told us we had value and worth," she began, "but we never under-stood what you meant until we read today that we were made in the image of God."

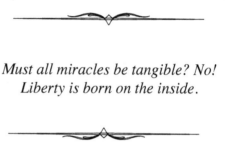

Must all miracles be tangible? No! Liberty is born on the inside.

It breaks the heart. Is there a more tragic subjugation among us than a woman or child manipulated or coerced into such a life—used and not loved—and then cruelly bound there by invisible chains of physical addiction and emotional intimidation? If so, it is difficult to imagine. These hurting among us are broken in every way.

Yet God works among the downtrodden and weary, those with no illusions of worldly grandeur. He sends His servants equipped with a heart of compassion, a resolve to rescue, and the hope of a redemption shining brilliantly before those emerging from dungeons of dejection. How beautiful the moment when the life lived with head bowed low in humil-iation and despair looks up and sees the reflection of God in the mirror. Must all miracles be tangible? No! Liberty is born on the inside.

While very few of us have been stripped of our freedoms as have these modern-day slaves among us, all of us are born into another kind of captivity from which we cannot free ourselves—our enslavement to sin for it, too, is an invisible bondage of the soul. And the outward expression of our inward condition has no bearing on our need for rescue and release. As Jesus taught us in the parable of the prodigal son, the soul of the smug is no less sin-steeped than the heart of the rebellious. We all need to be redeemed from sin and its power over us—to be restored to the way God made us to be.

Who can release us from oppression other than Him who has overcome our oppressor, and who then can make us new but Him who formed us in the first place? Who would even care enough to restore us if not Him who treasures us as His own? It was Christ himself, the Word of God, who came and lived among us to pay the price for our release from condemnation and to eternal life with God. Paul summarized plainly what God has done for us: "For he has rescued us from the dominion of darkness and brought us into the kingdom of the Son he loves, in whom we have redemption, the forgiveness of sins."[13]

No matter how we have lived life, we must be rescued from the power of sin and the consequences of our

---

[13] Colossians 1:13, 14

wrongdoing. No matter what we have done, Christ has paid for our sins. No matter who we are, we need only to trust in Christ, that He has purchased for us our redemption forever. In Him, we have value; we have worth.

He poured out his life unto death, and was numbered with the transgressors. For he bore the sin of many, and made intercession for the transgressors. (Isaiah 53:12)

Restored at a Price

I t was Augustine of Hippo who confessed, "You have made us for yourself, and our hearts are restless until they can find peace in you."[14] He certainly spoke for me. In fact, so restless was I one Sunday evening years ago that I called my mother to vent my frustration. "Mom, over the past ten years, I've prayed, read the Bible, gone to church, and begged and pleaded with God; but I'm just not getting it." She listened patiently to my lament and then responded, "I hear you speak of God, but I don't hear you mention Jesus." And with so few words, she had gotten to the crux of the matter.

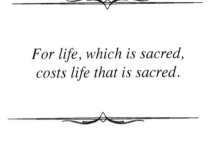

For life, which is sacred, costs life that is sacred.

"That's a sore spot with me," I replied, "I know the Bible teaches salvation comes through Jesus' death and resurrection, but I don't understand why. Why all the drama? Why couldn't He have just clicked his heels together three times and that be good enough?" (It somehow seemed like a plausible alternative at the time.) Now my mother had been a Bethel Bible Series teacher, and so she summarized the two-year course for me in about five minutes! She shared Leviticus 17:11, where God made it clear that ". . . the life of the creature is in the

---

[14] Augustine, Saint Bishop of Hippo, The Confessions of Saint Augustine, trans. Rex Warner. (New York: The New American Library, 1963), 17.

blood . . . it is the blood that makes atonement for one's life."
In other words, it takes one life to redeem another life lost.

Then, pulling it all together, Mom said, "In the Old
Testament, it was the blood of bulls and goats that was shed
for atonement, but that was only a foreshadowing of what was
to come. After all, how many goats are you worth? Only God's
life is able to save our life, which was made in His image. Jesus
sacrificed His perfect life to pay for our imperfect ones."

At the heart of redemption is this: Jesus "gave himself for
us to redeem us from all wickedness and to purify for himself
a people that are his very own."[15] We are so treasured, and He
loves us that much! For life, which is sacred, costs life that
is sacred. No other currency spends in the Kingdom of God.
No other funds are sufficient. Jesus' blood—Jesus' life—is
required and nothing less.

Everything clicked. After saying our goodbyes and hanging
up the phone, I went to my room, knelt beside my bed, and
entrusted my life to Jesus and His payment for my sins.

And, redeemed, I have rested well.

> *For you know that it was not with perishable*
> *things such as silver or gold that you were*
> *redeemed from the empty way of life . . . but*
> *with the precious blood of Christ, a lamb*
> *without blemish or defect. (1 Peter 1:18, 19)*

---

[15] Titus 2:14

From One Extreme to Another—and Back

P eggy and I were in awe as we entered the Vatican's Sistine Chapel. Like most tourists, we of course hastened to the center to lift our eyes and marvel at Michelangelo's iconic "The Creation of Adam" floating on the ceiling above us. We took in as much as we could in the insufficient time we had, including the rendering of "The Last Judgment," so compelling that we, like the others gathered before it, seemed almost unable to break away from its draw.

In the corner of the ceiling, to the right of the altar wall, was one small section left untouched during the magnificent restoration of the Chapel's frescos several years prior. Bearing still the accumulated dirt and soot of hundreds of years, it stood in stark contrast to the beautiful redemption of the artist's works. Were it not for the brightness of the restoration, we could not have comprehended the extent of degrading darkness; but for the grime, however, we would not have appreciated the full glory of the master's original artwork or its brilliant renewal.

In a sense, this contrast reminds us of another defilement and restoration. While the image of God can still be seen beneath the soil and stain of our sin, the tainted nature of a fallen people does not even come close to reflecting the splendor and care in which He created us. For in us God reflected His glory with bold, bright brushstrokes of light. Who can begin to fathom the value of God's own likeness painted on human canvas? Or who, for that matter, is able to measure depreciation from something of inestimable worth?

Then, can we even begin to imagine God's delight over a redeemed us? We indeed have been purchased, bought back at the greatest cost and restored in splendor to the Master Painter, reunited with Him through Christ. "I in them and you in me,"[16] petitioned Jesus to his Father on our behalf. It is so easy to view redemption from a distance, as though it were an object cordoned off behind museum ropes—something to study, but not touch. But it is not. Redemption is the work of a Friend who restores to His likeness the masterpiece He brought forth in His image in the first place.

We are this treasure! Perhaps one day we will finally understand the glory of our creation, the extent of our deface-ment, and the miracle of our restoration. Until then, we accept in faith that we are, to God, priceless.

> *For as high as the heavens are above the earth, so great is his love for those who fear him; as far as the east is from the west, so far has he removed our transgressions from us. (Psalm 103:11, 12)*

---

[16] John 17:23

Redeemed and with Purpose

There is a lot to like about growing up in a small town: the true sense of community, a slower pace of life, knowing most people, and the great outdoors. Yet for all its advantages, small-town living has its drawbacks and perhaps the foremost is this: reputations, once established, die hard. Some folks are ever-associated with their achievements and their feats, while

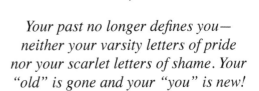

Your past no longer defines you— neither your varsity letters of pride nor your scarlet letters of shame. Your "old" is gone and your "you" is new!

others carry with them their indiscretions and mistakes. Varsity letters and scarlet letters—both are earned early and worn long.

But maybe a small town is just a big microscope. Maybe we're all indelibly defined—and confined—by fading glories of yesterday or by judgment errors along our way. Even if we were to relocate and start anew, could we ever escape ourselves—with our tendencies, our limitations, our memories, and our weaknesses?

Here's the good news. There actually is a place where we can restart, where we can be completely and continually new; and we needn't uproot to go there. The apostle Paul pointed out the way to this sure and certain hope of newness. What he wrote to the Corinthian church is penned to us all, "Therefore, if anyone is in Christ, he is a new creation; the old has gone, the new has come!"[17]

Pause for a moment. Read that again out loud or ponder it quietly. Take in its beauty and savor its hope. If you have entrusted your life to Christ alone, then "new creation" is true of you, for His Spirit is in you. Your past no longer defines you—neither your varsity letters of pride nor your scarlet letters of shame. Your "old" is gone and your "you" is new!

As people are made new in Christ, so too do we live with fresh purpose: to bring this message of reconciliation to the world around us—that God no longer counts people's sins against them.[18] The division between God and people has been bridged; a world scattered in sin can gather in redemption. God delights in us, His people, and we can rejoice in Him, our God.

> *And they sang a new song: "You are worthy to take the scroll and to open its seals, because you were slain, and with your blood you purchased men for God from every tribe and language and people and nation."*
> *(Revelation 5:9)*

---

[17] 2 Corinthians 5:17
[18] 2 Corinthians 5:18, 19

3

Christ in me Is Freedom

By nature, I am captive, but there is no captivity in Christ.
Christ is my life, and Christ in me is freedom.

Freedom from; Freedom To

*T*he *Karate Kid* is a feel-good movie about a bullied teenager who, with the help of his aging friend, Mr. Miyagi, prepares to face his tormentors. Mr. Miyagi agrees to instruct Daniel in the martial art in exchange for help with some tedious tasks—waxing his cars, painting his house and fence, and sanding his floors. The daily duties commence as planned, but the combat training seems not to. When Daniel finally loses his patience and accuses him of reneging on his promise, Mr. Miyagi shows him that, through the exacting motions required to execute each chore, Daniel has indeed acquired basic karate skills without even knowing it! He is liberated from his defenselessness and able to stand up to his foe.

We, too, have been liberated from helplessness—in our case, a spiritual one—for God has poured Himself into us and equipped us to face down our enemy. But like the young man in the movie, we don't *feel* any different until we *see* we are changed; we don't *realize* our empowerment until we *consider* it with new understanding. How does our experience change when, through the eyes of belief, we see beyond the way things appear and live instead in faith? What does life look like when we approach it as people transformed? From what oppression have we been released, and to what victories have we been freed?

Alive in Christ and our minds set on Him, we are:

free from belittling others in attempts to elevate ourselves by comparison, and
free to see them as people like us, fellow sojourners in need of grace;

free from envy over what we do not have, and
free to celebrate with others the gifts God distributes as He pleases;

free from conforming to the expectations of others in search of approval, and
free to be who God made us to be and to thrive in Him;

free from enslavement to the cycle of retaliation, and
free to respond in peace and grace to those who offend us;

free from wandering aimless paths of our own making, and
free to follow in faith the ways of God, illumined by His Word;

free from Satan's harsh accusations of fault, and
free to trust in the Spirit's care as He sculpts us into the likeness of Christ;

free from uncertainty of our eternal destiny, and
free to share with others our sure and certain hope of salvation in Christ;

free from clutching the "things" we will one day leave behind, and

free to build up treasures that await us when we rise in Him.

If you hold to my teaching, you are really my disciples. Then you will know the truth, and the truth will set you free. (John 8:31, 32)

A Stockholm Syndrome of the Soul

I n 1973, Swedish robbers held several bank employees captive for six days. It's not as though these criminals were searching for new, meaningful relationships; rather it was for their own purposes they robbed these innocents of their freedom. Yet in an odd twist of events, the employees, though exploited in this way, developed a curious, emotional attachment to their captors, defending them even after they were arrested! Since that time, a captive's irrational bond to his captor has come to be known as "the Stockholm Syndrome."

The apostle James warned of a similar kidnapping, a seizing of the soul by which each one of us is "dragged away and enticed" by the unlikeliest of bullies, our own "evil desire."[19] The truth be told, our capture is not really all that difficult, for personal gratification is actually quite alluring to that part of us that wants to live life on our own terms and for our own pleasure. ("No need to drag me away, Mr. Desire. I go willingly!")

But Evil Desire is not our friend, and our attraction to him is anything but rational. In fact, he mocks us, his captives, as he tantalizes us down the path to wrongdoing. He may bankroll our greed, for instance, but just enough to keep us ever wanting more. He may feed our starving egos but never satisfies our pride. He may set us up with the object of our

---

[19] James 1:14

wandering eye, but we wake up to realize lust was a far cry from the love we exchanged for it. He suggests lies to utter for the sake of convenience and then more lies to cover up and perpetuate our deceptions. One day we find ourselves someplace we never thought we'd be: completely helpless, unable to resist Evil Desire, and bound up by our sin.

There is a way out, however; God has not abandoned us. Though we followed Evil Desire into captivity by our own volition, "gratifying the cravings of our sinful nature and following its desires and thoughts,"[20] it was Christ who "gave himself as a ransom for all men,"[21] paying the consequences of our sin and freeing us from its grasp. Then to all who trust in Him, Jesus sends the Spirit as a guide, a fresh voice with good counsel. This Spirit of God will never entice us to do wrong but reliably points us down the paths that are good and right. His ways are clearly distinguished, for His desires are always contrary to the evil desires of our sinful nature.[22] Ours is to follow this voice, offering ourselves entirely to Him with open and submitted hearts.

We all face temptations in life, and their allure is strong; this will never change on this side of eternity. We no longer need to cower before them in weakness or acquiesce to their harsh demands, however, for the irrational bond to our captor

---

[20] Ephesians 2:3
[21] 1 Timothy 2:6
[22] Galatians 5:17

has been broken. We are as free as the Spirit of God who lives within us.

Now the Lord is the Spirit, and where the Spirit of the Lord is, there is freedom. (2 Corinthians 3:17)

Rejecting Rejection

The older I get, the more I appreciate "throw away the mold" kinds of people. You know, the ones who are unlike anyone else you've ever met. They seem refreshingly unfettered by conformity, living instead in the uniqueness of who they are. If the opinions of others matter to them, it certainly doesn't show through personal constraint! No, these gems stand out like pearls in a jeweler's tray of rubies.

Most of us are more conventional, bending our appearance, our actions, and our speech to the unspoken expectations of others. Our desire for approval tempers our expression of individuality. For the Christian, the divide between who we are and the norms of society is even greater, for we have come to exalt God's ways that are so different than our own. We are, as Peter observed, "strangers in the world."[23] Sadly, in order to "fit in," then, we stifle our identity, in part

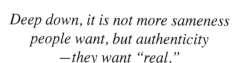

Deep down, it is not more sameness people want, but authenticity — they want "real."

concealing Christ who lives in us, which is a shame because, in so doing, we miss amazing opportunities to impact the world around us in profound and eternal ways. Deep down, it is not more sameness people want, but authenticity — they want "real." People search for liberty in life and certainty in

---

[23] 1 Peter 1:1

truth. They seek light in their darkness; they crave water for their dryness.

Aren't all of these things found in Christ? Haven't we discovered in Him the treasures we all dream about—goodness and kindness, fullness and hope, forgiveness and faithfulness, and mercy and grace? There is no "same old, same old" about Jesus, only fulfillment ever fresh.

How tragic it is when we, in faintness of heart, obscure Jesus before a people longing to behold Him in an unencumbered view. He lives in us not as one to be constrained in our weakness of character, but as one to be proclaimed in the freedom of rebirth in Christ.

When it comes down to it, binding ourselves to the expectations of others is one of the greatest obstacles to our effectiveness as Jesus' followers. We are accepted, loved, and treasured by the God who knows everything there is to know about us, free to "shine like stars in the universe as [we] hold out the word of life."[24] Then overflowing in this grace, let us exude the life, truth, and love of Christ, not defensively or fearfully, but eagerly and gladly. Let us leave behind our timid pursuit of conditional approval and, instead, strive to show people the full and eternal acceptance *they* will find in Christ.

> *Fear of man will prove to be a snare, but whoever trusts in the Lord is kept safe. (Proverbs 29:25)*

---

[24] Philippians 2:15, 16

Who Captures Whom?

I t is always a feel-good story—the oppressed is released from captivity and ascends to a position of authority, there governing in fairness, honor, mercy, and grace. We cheer for righted wrongs. Take Joseph, for instance. Heartlessly sold by his brothers and unjustly jailed by his master, he ultimately found favor in the eyes of Pharaoh and was placed second in command of all Egypt. There he exercised his responsibilities with conviction, wisdom, and great care. Goodness triumphed. The hero won. The people flourished.

There was a time when we were powerless to break free from the control of our own passions. Our desires, said Paul, double-crossed us as "the trap of the devil," taking us "captive to do his will."[25] But Christ has released us from our bondage and, as He himself said, "If the Son sets you free, you will be free indeed."[26] The captive status of yesterday defines us no more, and we are no longer caged by the trapper.

Then how do once-held individuals thrive as a people now-free? Certainly Satan still tempts us toward disbelief and deceives us into disobedience. So how do we stand strong in the face of this one before whom we once cowered, and how do we resist the allure that mocks our weakness?

When tempted by Satan in the wilderness, Jesus destroyed his deceptions with what he knew to be true: the Word of God.

---

[25] 2 Timothy 2:26
[26] John 8:36

When Jesus agonized in Gethsemane, he submitted himself to what he knew to be right: the will of God. This is the same Christ who lives in us today, the one who sent His Spirit to remind us of His words and to guide us in the ways of God that are written on our hearts.

Then is it any wonder, when engaged in spiritual battle, Paul followed Jesus' lead in turning the tables on our enemy? "We demolish arguments and every pretension that sets itself up against the knowledge of God," he proclaimed, "and we take captive every thought to make it obedient to Christ."[27]

So now who captures whom? We are no longer captives to sin; we have become its captors.

---

[27] 2 Corinthians 10:5

4

Christ in Me Is Confidence

By nature, I am fearful, but there is no fear in Christ.
Christ is my life, and Christ in me is confidence.

No Less God Today

I love growing older. I really do. Easy to say, perhaps, because I've not yet reached the point of deteriorating health, but the perspective that comes with age is wonderful!

Stop and look back on your life. No matter what age you are, stop and look back. Can you now see evidence of the invisible hand of God faithfully guiding you through every step of your journey? It might be fascinating to make a list of His works in your life. Who did God send to you with the truth of salvation in Christ? Who responded to His call to teach and nurture you in understanding and wisdom? When did God protect you from—or lead you through—physical danger? How did He sustain you in—or deliver you from—unhealthy relationships? What strength or character did He build into your spirit amid your toughest trials? When did God bandage your wounded soul and carry you through internal struggles? How many times has He surprised you with blessings for which you never even thought to ask?

Maybe He led you around a problem, avoiding certain calamity. More often, likely, He ushered you right through opposition or trouble. Like Daniel's friends in the furnace or Daniel himself in the lions' den, you weren't spared the difficult experience, but you endured it and emerged from it even stronger through the power of Him who is sovereign over all things and in all circumstances. Who knows the number of times God has protected us without our even knowing we were in danger? And through it all, He's loosened our white-knuckled grip on self-reliance and firmed up our faith in Him. We naturally fear what we cannot control and, truth be told, we can't control much. We can be confident, though, for the God whose presence we see through the clarity of hindsight is no less with us today. The God who has guided and supported us every step along the way is no less faithful today. The God who delivered us in the past is no less powerful today. His love truly does endure forever, so in a day yet to come, we will look back on this one and proclaim He was no less God today.

Then I thought, "To this I will appeal: the years of the right hand of the Most High." I will remember the deeds of the Lord; yes, I will remember your miracles of long ago. I will meditate on all your works and consider all your mighty deeds. (Psalm 77:10–12)

Can Do and Will Do

At the most basic level, interviewing job seekers always comes down to assessing two things: their "can do" and their "will do." The former refers to a person's ability to learn job demands and perform them to expectations; the latter relates to his or her commitment to doing well. The ideal candidate excels in both areas. Over the years, I have interviewed hundreds of people, each time attempting to evaluate these two qualities in them. How ironic then, when it comes to working in the Kingdom of God, I find myself naturally short-suited in both departments! Jesus' words summarize my own "can do" honestly enough: "apart from me you can do nothing."[28] Concerning the "will do" of my sinful nature, His words ring true again, "Why do you call me, 'Lord, Lord,' and do not do what I say?"[29] If I were to interview myself on behalf of Father & Son, Inc., I wouldn't get an offer! Truth be told, none of us would be up to the task. No "can do" plus no "will do" equals no job.

But God hires us anyway! Then He generously invests in us, pouring himself into us and equipping us for the good works He has in mind for us to do. Certainly, Paul recognized where his "can do" came from: "I can do all things through him who strengthens me."[30] The apostle understood

---

[28] John 15:5
[29] Luke 6:46
[30] Philippians 4:13 (ESV)

our ability for God's work comes from Christ, as does our strength for it. Through Him and by His power at work in us, our Kingdom work is productive.

As for the "will do"? Again, Paul observed it arises not from ourselves, but from God, who works in us "both to will and to work for his good pleasure."[31] It is God who equips us for our calling, and it is He who inspires us with commitment, desire, eagerness, and zeal.

God didn't merely hire us into His Kingdom; He recruited us, and He paid dearly to bring us into His Company. Then He gave us His Word—His training manual—so that we may be "thoroughly equipped for every good work."[32]

Every task He has prepared for us matters for eternity. How's *that* for job satisfaction?

If a man remains in me and I in him, he will bear much fruit. (John 15:5)

---

[31] Philippians 2:13 (ESV)
[32] 2 Timothy 3:17

Truth and Appearances

W ho can forget the 1989 image of a solitary protester in Tiananmen Square, whose mere presence and conviction brought a roaring army tank to a complete standstill? Fortified both in strength of steel and the authority of the Chinese government, this massive, advancing behemoth lost its battle against one man literally standing for freedom and armed only in courage. Appearances deceived that day; power wasn't as it seemed.

The apostle Paul found himself in a similar circumstance—a lone figure, facing the "machinery" of Judea. Convened to hear Paul defend his ministry were King Herod Agrippa and his sister Bernice, Governor Festus, and a room full of military officers and local leaders. At the command of Agrippa, Paul was brought into the auditorium. Bound with chains, he stood before them, alone.

It was a display of authority that would intimidate just about anyone, but Paul would not be snared by fear, for this moment was opportunity, not only for his defense, but more so for witness to God's faithfulness to His promises. Paul needed no weapons, for he was already armed with all the power he needed—the knowledge and assurance of truth. In this confidence, he clearly and concisely explained both his hope in the long-promised Messiah and his faith in Jesus, who fulfilled all the Messianic predictions of the prophets.

At that point, it became clear where the real power lay and where it did not. It was Festus, the governor, who first lost composure, shouting "Paul, you are out of your mind!" ("I am not out of my mind . . . but I utter words of sober truth. For the king knows about these matters, and I speak to him also with confidence . . ."[33]) Then when Paul asked Agrippa if he believed in the prophets, this most powerful man in the room dodged the question by scoffing at the notion of becoming a Christian. Like the tank in Beijing, these leaders veered right and then veered left, but Paul remained confidently before them in truth. Outgunned, the king stood and left the room in full retreat, dignitaries in tow. Those who entered the room with great pomp left it, well, pomp-less! Only when out of earshot did Agrippa privately confess, "This man is not doing anything worthy of death or imprisonment."[34]

It is only natural to fear what meets the eye. Like Paul, we do well to place our confidence in "sober truth," for the Christ who claimed to be truth itself lives within us.

> *The one who is in you is greater than the one who is in the world. (1 John 4:4)*

---

[33] Acts 26:24–26 (NASB)
[34] Acts 26:31 (NASB)

Extraordinary Power in Ordinary People

T hink about the people who have made the most profound impacts on your life. I'll bet, for you, it was a distinguished senator who told you about God's love for you in Christ Jesus. No? Well, then maybe it was a Fortune 500 CEO who prayed with you through your toughest trial, right? No? OK, then it must have been an Ivy League professor who was there when you really needed words of wisdom! Wrong again?

Perhaps the most endearing thing about the Kingdom of God is its ragtag constituency. Stop for a moment and note the few people who have made the biggest difference in your life. Finished? OK, now see how your list coincides with Paul's observation of the early church. "Not many . . . were wise by human

Perhaps the most endearing thing about the Kingdom of God is its ragtag constituency.

standards; not many were influential; not many were of noble birth."[35] Does this match the list of those who have ministered most to you? It does, mine! In fact, when the seventy-two disciples Jesus sent out to perform wonders in His name returned with great reports, Jesus rejoiced in the Spirit and praised

---

[35] 1 Corinthians 1:26

His Father for having "hidden these things from the wise and learned"[36] and revealing them instead to ordinary people.

When it comes to ministering to others, we tend to look at ourselves and see only our natural insufficiency. What we need to realize is God intentionally chose us—the "foolish," the "weak," the "lowly," and the "despised."[37] Why? It is because the power of God shows mightier through the weak, for what other explanation is there but God himself? The wisdom of God is more confounding when it passes through the lips of those dismissed as the simple among us. It is because God is magnified through those who, though despised, love anyway; and the delight of God leaps in the hearts of the humble.

We ought not curse our shortcomings, but rejoice in them, for Christ is most glorified when He makes competent a humble people who rely entirely on Him.

Such confidence as this is ours through Christ before God. Not that we are competent in ourselves to claim anything for ourselves, but our competence comes from God. He has made us competent as ministers of a new covenant. (2 Corinthians 3:4–6)

---

[36] Luke 10:21
[37] 1 Corinthians 1:27, 28

5

Christ in Me Is Salvation

By nature, I am condemned,
but there is no condemnation in Christ.
Christ is my life, and Christ in me is salvation.

Jesus Seeks

A re you a t-shirt reader? Do bumper stickers draw your attention? Do you look at church signs as you drive by them? If so, then you have seen the message, "Jesus saves." Even if you know little or nothing about Christianity, "Jesus saves" is likely a familiar refrain to you. Yet when we move beyond the sound bite and examine the gospel message behind it, we find that, before Jesus saves, Jesus seeks. He seeks us. In fact, He seeks us intently.

How important is it to Jesus that people know and understand His seeking heart? When a group of Pharisees muttered among themselves about Jesus engaging the spiritual outcasts of the day, He told them in no uncertain terms—through three consecutive parables—it was these very "sinners" whom He had come to call back to Himself. Like a shepherd leaving ninety-nine sheep to find the lost one, like a woman scouring her house for a missing coin, and like a father scanning the horizon for his wayward son, God searches for those who are apart from Him.

It's not as though Jesus doesn't know where we are; He does. Yet history shows we are perfectly capable of shutting God out, even when He reveals Himself to us in jaw-dropping ways. When Jesus miraculously healed the sick on the Sabbath, how did the religious leaders respond but to accuse Him of breaking the moral law? After God performed miracle after miracle to extricate His enslaved people from Egypt, how did they react to threatening circumstances but to beg Moses to escort them back there?

So Jesus calls to us in ways only our hearts can hear. How deeply moving is it, for instance, to receive kindness and care from another who expects nothing in return,

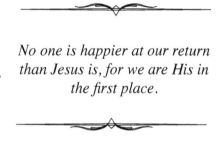

No one is happier at our return than Jesus is, for we are His in the first place.

especially when that person is a total stranger? Have you ever noticed "something different" about a person, later to discover it was the joy and peace of Christ shining out from within? Have you ever heard stories of non-believers who startled themselves by calling out to God in a moment of crisis? And sometimes we just reach the end of ourselves—weary and disillusioned—only to find God there with us, just as He had been all along.

When we finally hear Jesus' voice and turn to Him, what fills our vision but His wide-open arms eager to embrace us and carry us home? No one is happier at our return than Jesus is, for we are His in the first place. We gratefully experience salvation from the vantage point of the endangered sheep, but He celebrates our return as the One who cares enough to leave everything behind to come and find us. "I tell you," He said, ". . . there will be more rejoicing in heaven over one sinner who repents than over ninety-nine righteous persons who do not need to repent." [38]

---

[38] Luke 15:7

Jesus seeks. Jesus saves. Jesus celebrates!

Rejoice with me; I have found my lost sheep.
(Luke 15:6)

One Man after Another

C hildren are naturally adept at making messes, aren't they? Supply them with any arsenal of raw materials—flour and eggs, crayons and markers, dirt and mud—and they will showcase an ability to create disorder of impressive proportions. But they all grow out of it, right? We wish! On the contrary, the muddy messes we made as children are nothing compared to the colossal chaos we create as adults. We who once spilled milk onto kitchen counters and floors grew up to spill oil into the earth's oceans and seas. The scribbles we left all over our parents' walls pale in comparison to the chemicals we released into the skies above. Bigger kids make bigger spills, and it doesn't take many of us to do it!

There has never been, however, a catastrophe such as that of one man, Adam. He was the jewel in a creation of only goodness; he lived and ruled in a place where all was as it should be. It was the kind of world for which we clamor when we decry what is. Yet despite God's clear command to the contrary, Adam nevertheless sought to know both good and evil. Though specifically warned, he chose death. It was a disaster incalculable in magnitude. Like a nuclear explosion contaminating water, land, and air far beyond our horizon, Adam's choice polluted the entirety of a pristine creation made to be "very good." It was the cataclysmic event that led to all others.

As vast the earthly devastation that can occur from the error of a mere few, it is even more incomprehensible the thought of one person being able to reverse the damage. Can we imagine, for example, being tasked with single-handedly cleaning up radioactive contamination? We laugh at a thought so ridiculous. Yet this is precisely what one man, Jesus, did: He cleaned up Adam's mess! Paul wrote, "Just as the result of one trespass was condemnation for all men, so also the result of one act of righteousness was justification that brings life for all men. For just as through the disobedience of the one man the many were made sinners, so also through the obedience of the one man the many will be made righteous."[39]

When our sin was beyond measure and we had no hope, Jesus did what no one else could do: He cleaned us up and saved us to Himself. What remains for us? Thank Him with our reclaimed lives.

He saved us through the washing of rebirth and renewal by the Holy Spirit, whom he poured out on us generously through Jesus Christ our Savior, so that, having been justified by his grace, we might become heirs having the hope of eternal life. (Titus 3:5–7)

---

[39] Romans 5:18, 19

A Complete Salvation

Certainly the most enduring images of the 1989 oil spill in Prince William Sound are those of its helpless victims—sea animals and waterfowl covered with crude. Still today we occasionally see pictures of ducks, geese, and other birds unable to fly or, in many cases, even to escape the grip of the caramel-like substance released from its confines. A slow starvation awaited most of them. Yet standing out against the drab backdrop of black and brown shores were the bright spots of salvation—rescue workers tirelessly giving of themselves to deliver grounded birds from their open-air graves. After freeing captive fowl, these caregivers gently scrubbed feathers free of impurities. Then having cleansed them, they released their winged patients to soar again as they were made to soar. It was a complete salvation—rescue, yes, and remediation and release, as well. Tragedy was turned to triumph.

Our salvation is likewise a process. It was not an environmental event that ensnared us, but an inner guilt from which we could not escape, no matter how hard we tried. But the caring Christ sought us out and, finding us mired in contamination, reached down and pulled us up out of the grip of filth. He hid our lives safely in His and brought us with Him into right standing before God. *In Christ, we were justified.*

We were plucked out of our pollution, but our salvation did not end there, for God continues to cleanse us so that we will again look as we were created to look and to do as we were designed to do. Though pain is part of the process, He works with us to strengthen our faith in Him and deepen our love. In this way, we "are receiving the goal of [our] faith, the salvation of [our] souls."[40] *In Christ, we are being sanctified.*

There will be a day when Christ returns, "to bring salvation to those who are waiting for him."[41] Our cleansing will be complete, and John says, "We shall be like him."[42] Paul echoes, "When Christ, who is your life, appears, then you also will appear with him in glory."[43] On that day we will be raised up to the heavens by fresh winds under outstretched wings. *In Christ, we will be glorified.*

In Christ, we are picked up, cleaned up, and raised up—justified, sanctified, and glorified. We are now and forever saved.

> *And you also were included in Christ when you heard the word of truth, the gospel of your salvation. Having believed, you were marked in him with a seal, the promised Holy Spirit, who is a deposit guaranteeing our inheritance until the redemption of those who are God's possession—to the praise of his glory. (Ephesians 1:13, 14)*

---

[40] 1 Peter 1:9
[41] Hebrews 9:28
[42] 1 John 3:2
[43] Colossians 3:4

Faith-Sharing for the Rest of Us

> *Then Peter, filled with the Holy Spirit said*
> *to them: " . . . Salvation is found in no one*
> *else, for there is no other name under heaven*
> *given to men by which we must be saved."*
> *(Acts 4:8, 12)*

May I be honest with you? "Bold" just doesn't come naturally to me. I wish it did, but it does not. I stroll through the Boldness Hall of Fame and see Peter and Paul. Over here is Barnabas and—look—there's Stephen! I also know several people today who'd get my vote as future inductees, but me? . . . Let's just say no one has asked me to pose for a bust.

I sincerely hope "bold" describes you. If so, please know I join the many brothers and sisters in Christ who look up to you. This discussion is for the rest of us, but you're more than welcome to eavesdrop if you wish.

True confession: For many years, Jesus' "great commission" has been not so much inspiration for me but, rather, intimidation. The command to "go and make disciples" has stirred more anxiety in the stomach than eagerness in the heart. I'd much rather *be* a disciple than go out and *make* one. More recently, this has begun to change, which is God's doing, not mine. I have found no spiritual silver bullets for faith-sharing, but I have picked up a few golden nuggets of grace along the way. I share these not as a formula or a checklist and especially not as rules. Rather they are perspectives conveyed in the hope that some may be of help to others.

Remember. Do you recall what your life was like before you discovered Jesus to be real—your search, your emptiness, your confusion? It helps to remember people all over the world still long to fill this familiar void in their soul.

Appreciate. Who shared Jesus with you, answered your questions, or walked patiently beside you on your path to Christ? Isn't it true these people still occupy a special place of warmth and gratitude in your heart today? While we fear rejection—and may experience it—many people will appreciate us for kindly speaking the truth about a loving, saving God.

Witnessing is one thing. What is a witness but one who simply tells what he or she has seen? People love to hear stories purely and enthusiastically shared from the heart. So tell the story of what God has done in your life. He will infuse it with hope.

Sharing is another. Our stories of what God has done in our lives may or may not lead to a discussion of God's plan salvation through Jesus Christ. In either case, we do well to be ready to share the gospel story with those who want to hear it. God will take it from there.

Decide to say "yes" to the Spirit. Our self-centered nature prefers we not risk ridicule by sharing Christ with others; the Spirit, on the other hand, urges us to proclaim Him. We do well to recognize the unseen argument within and to follow the Spirit's lead.

Look for open doors. Many times over the years, I've turned away from clear calls to witness, share, or serve and felt awful about it. Other times, I've tried to force my own opportunities and felt stupid. But isn't it exhilarating when we see a God-opened door, take a deep spiritual breath of trust, and then step into the moment? Those are the times we savor. Watch for them.

Know what only God can do; do only what he leads you to do. Only God can draw one's heart to Himself. Only He can breathe new life into a soul weary in its striving. Our role is simply to share our stories, explain the gospel or serve in Jesus' name—no less and no more than God is leading us in the moment. We leave the results to God, for only He can produce them.

Re-think "bold." It helps me to think of "bold" as eagerly executing my God-assigned task, confident He will turn it into something great in the life of another.

Define the enemy. We share Christ with another not as though in across-the-table negotiations, but shoulder-to-shoulder with a friend. Satan is the enemy and we speak truth in the face of his deceptions, trusting God's Word will prevail.

Be your sanctified you. God has planned all sorts of good works for us, and He equips each of us uniquely for them. We do well, then, to be content in how He has prepared us and expectant that He will work through us.

On our own, we can do nothing for the kingdom of God, absolutely nothing. But the Spirit in us can do much, and He will.

> *I am not ashamed of the gospel, because it is the power of God for the salvation of everyone who believes: first for the Jew, then for the Gentile. For in the gospel a righteousness from God is revealed, a righteousness that is by faith from first to last. (Romans 1:16, 17)*

6

Christ in Me Is Righteousness

By nature, I am sinful, but there is no sin in Christ.
Christ is my life, and Christ in me is righteousness.

I Must, but I Can't!

Have you ever found yourself in an "I must, but I can't" predicament? It occurs when we are expected to meet an objective or accomplish a task but lack the resources to do so. Whether short on time, staffing, funds, or skill, we stagger under the impossible burden only made heavier by the dissatisfaction of others and our own frustration in failure. When the Israelites were forced into the hard labor of brickmaking, for example, there came a time when their Egyptian captors added to their burden, forcing them to gather their own straw for the process while keeping their production demands the same. When the people failed to meet their now-impossible quotas, their foremen were beaten.

To the church in Rome, Paul described another "I must, but I can't" scenario. He said, "I know that nothing good lives in me, that is, in my sinful nature. For I have the desire to do what is good, but I cannot carry it out."[44] We can relate to his conundrum, can't we? Inside, we *want* to be as we ought to be; we *want* to be acceptable before God; we *want* to be guiltless before Him who knows everything about us. Which is to say we *want* to be righteous, but we are not, not on our own, anyway. Our issue is not one of physical incapacity but of spiritual inadequacy. We might want to do the right thing and keep God's law, but we cannot. In fact, His commands only point out how far we fall short of a God who

---

[44] Romans 7:18

will not compromise with sin as mankind has done. No, on the contrary, the "sinful mind," writes Paul, "does not submit to God's law, nor can it do so."[45]

But Jesus can! And Jesus did! "Tempted in all things as we are, yet without sin,"[46] He perfectly fulfilled God's law. Then being perfect, He willingly offered His life as a sacrifice for us, "in order that the righteous requirements of the law might be fully met in us, who do not live according to the sinful nature but according to the Spirit."[47] Paul writes, "Christ is the end of the law so that there may be righteousness for everyone who believes."[48]

We can stop pursuing the impossible task of justifying ourselves against God's commandments, for the only One who *could* keep them *did* keep them, and He lives in us. We can stop trying to become acceptable to God through our own efforts, for our righteousness is a person, Jesus Christ. In Him alone, we live forever in the presence of our holy God.

We can. We must.

But when the kindness and love of God our Savior appeared, he saved us, not because of righteous things we had done, but because of his mercy. (Titus 3:4)

---

[45] Romans 8:7
[46] Hebrews 4:15 (NASB)
[47] Romans 8:4
[48] Romans 10:4

The Books Are Closed

A good friend was reflecting back on an earlier period in his life, a difficult time of struggle for sobriety and inner peace. Adding pressure at the time were his moral failures, which left him feeling short on hope and long on self-pity. He said, "I finally came to the point where I had to fire that debit/credit god of mine." I chuckled at his description and understood what he meant. It was his rendezvous with the truth that, no matter how strong our desires or intentions to the contrary, doing wrong is inescapable and offsetting our wrongs, insurmountable. Try as he might, no amount of "plusses" could ever erase any amount of "minuses" in his "morality" account. Though he may not have articulated it this way at the time, he was beginning to realize his need for grace.

> *Though he may not have articulated it this way at the time, he was beginning to realize his need for grace.*

As His time on earth drew to an end, Jesus promised to send the Holy Spirit who would reveal our sin, not in harshness, but as a favor to us. As we come to terms with our own moral bankruptcy, the Spirit points us to Jesus, in whom we can find a right relationship with God, moreover, a righteous identity in God. For Jesus is the faultless one who holds forth His righteousness to us as a gift!

So what must we do? How do we accept this undeserved gift of infinite worth? God only requires from us what he received from Abraham: belief, our complete trust in Christ. Abraham "believed the Lord, and he credited it to him as righteousness."[49] For Abraham's faith was not vague or directionless, but very specifically placed in nothing less than "the gospel in advance."[50] Paul assures us God's blessing to Abraham extends also to all who believe in this gospel of Jesus Christ: "The words, 'it was credited to him' were written not for him alone, but also for us, to whom God will credit righteousness—for us who believe in him who raised Jesus our Lord from the dead."[51]

My friend was right. We need not obsess over the debits and credits of our sinful nature; our funds are sufficient in Christ. We need not fret in futility over our ledgers; our debts are canceled. And the books are closed.

The righteous will live by his faith.
(Habakkuk 2:4)

---

[49] Genesis 15:6
[50] Galatians 3:8
[51] Romans 4:23, 24

Free on the Inside!

Through years of prison ministry, I have heard several inmates reflect upon their incarceration as "the best thing that ever happened to me." While the law of the land had judged their actions and pronounced their guilt, it also brought them to the point of self-examination and discovery. It was there they confronted their lives and confessed their hearts, and it was there they were rendered righteous before God through faith in Jesus Christ.

Most of us have never faced justice inside the courtroom, yet our sin no less separates us from God than those who have. Do you recall, for instance, what Jesus said about being angry arising out of the same spiritual condition as murder?

So how does God respond to our offenses? He hands us over to the consequences of our choices. As the apostle Paul observed, "the Scripture declares that the whole world is a prisoner of sin."[52] Surely it pained God to see us forfeit our freedom. Yet like society's correctional institutions, which give their residents pause for introspection and time for self-assessment, the "prison of sin" leads all of us to our own moment of truth. Paul went on to explain we were all "held prisoners by the law," a jailer, of sorts, "put in charge to lead us to Christ that we might be justified by faith."[53] Having confronted us with the futility of our ways and their

---

[52] Galatians 3:22
[53] Galatians 3:23, 24

inescapable end, the law then points us to the only place we can be rectified to God and made right before Him.

Jesus is that place. The apostle John declared this great hope, "if anybody does sin, we have one who speaks to the Father in our defense—Jesus Christ, the Righteous One. He is the atoning sacrifice for our sins, and not only for ours but also for the sins of the whole world."[54] As Jesus intercedes on our behalf, the Father ascribes His righteousness to us. So great is His love for His Son; so great is His love for us.

God's law will never declare us "not guilty." Instead, it escorts us always to Christ, where we find mercy and grace and forgiveness and acceptance from God. It is in this sure and certain hope that we can join the declaration of our brothers and sisters behind bars, "I'm free on the inside."

> *What is more, I consider everything a loss compared to the surpassing greatness of knowing Christ Jesus my Lord, for whose sake I have lost all things. I consider them rubbish, that I may gain Christ and be found in him, not having a righteousness of my own that comes from the law, but that which is through faith in Christ—the righteousness that comes from God and is by faith. (Philippians 3:8, 9)*

---

[54] 1 John 2:1, 2

Living Righteousness

S uppose two people donated money to a cause; one felt compelled to give out of obligation or social pressure, but the other eagerly poured out her gift, matching it dollar for dollar with hope. Which heart mirrored God's heart? Imagine one man did a good deed in order to feel good about himself, while another served in empathy, love, and compassion. Who do you think reflected the character of Christ?

Speaking to a large number of His followers one day, Jesus said, "Unless your righteousness surpasses that of the Pharisees and the teachers of the law, you will certainly not enter the kingdom of heaven."[55] It must have confounded the people, for the Pharisees were passionate about keeping the law for the very purpose of establishing favor with God. It's who they were; it's what they did. How could anyone possibly exceed their righteousness?

"Their righteousness" was precisely their problem, for the Pharisees' version of it was a distant cry from God's. The Israelites "did not know the righteousness that comes from God and sought to establish their own," wrote Paul, himself a former Pharisee, "They did not submit to God's righteousness."[56] They "pursued it not by faith but as if it were by works."[57] No wonder Jesus pointed to a higher standard!

---

[55] Matthew 5:20
[56] Romans 10:3
[57] Romans 9:32

By now we know the doctrine. We know we "must" be as we ought to be, but on our own, we "can't." We know God accepts to Himself all who trust in Christ, and He closes the books, eliminating the moral debits we have amassed, plus the credits we *think* we have earned. We know that because our righteousness is a person—Christ in us—we are "free on the inside." So why do we still struggle with this precious gift so lovingly given? "Saved," we savor; "forgiven," we welcome. But "righteous"? It can be difficult to accept.

We must trust with our lives the grace we confess. Though righteousness might be the last thing we'd ever ascribe to ourselves, the fact of the matter is, God has declared it of all in whom Christ lives by faith. So we step into a new identity freely given and humbly received, and we give ourselves over to Him entirely as His "instruments of righteousness."[58]

So what does it look like to offer ourselves to God for his purposes? We live life glorifying God, rather than justifying ourselves. We openly confess our wrongs to the One who paid our penalty, rather than concealing them for fear of retribution. We serve in humility, knowing we live in imputed virtue undeserved. We give grace to others, rather than holding them to a standard we could not attain ourselves. We show mercy, knowing we have been deemed just. And we point others to the gift that awaits all who believe—the righteousness of Christ.

---

[58] Romans 6:13

And this is my prayer: that your love may abound more and more in knowledge and depth of insight, so that you may be able to discern what is best and may be pure and blameless until the day of Christ, filled with the fruit of righteousness that comes through Jesus Christ—to the glory and praise of God. (Philippians 1:9–11)

7

Christ in Me Is Strength

By nature, I am weak, but there is no weakness in Christ.
Christ is my life, and Christ in me is strength.

Strength in Weakness

Anyone who pulls out a club and tees up the ball soon learns the agonizing truth that golf is "the game of opposites." When the club head passes through on a leftward trajectory, the ball "slices" to the right; when the pendulum swings right, the ball "hooks" left. If we want the shot to go higher, we don't scoop underneath the ball, rather we swing down on it. But most of all, to hit the ball farther, we must relax our grip and (repeat after me) *slow down!* It is the smooth, easy swing that powers the longer, stronger golf shot. It's all so counterintuitive! It's so frustrating—yet so true!

And it is so similar to living strong in the Spirit! For the less we cling to our own will and the less we insist on our own way, the more powerfully the Spirit of God flows in us and through us. Jesus has coached us in this "opposites" principle clearly enough: "My power is made perfect in weakness."[59] Ever His student, the apostle Paul attested, ". . . when I am weak, then I am strong."[60] The concept is hardly new, but it is a consistent truth throughout the Biblical narrative. It wasn't the forty-year-old, "kill-a-man-with-my-bare-hands" Moses who led Israel out of Egypt, but an older, weaker Moses, now "more humble than anyone else on the face of the earth."[61] And what mighty warrior did God commission to save Israel from the

---

[59] 2 Corinthians 12:9
[60] 2 Corinthians 12:10
[61] Numbers 12:3

Midianites but Gideon, the runt of the litter in the weakest clan of Manasseh! (Who, me?)

On its face, it seems so unnatural that God would choose to exhibit His strength through our weakness. Then again, if "the weakness of God is stronger than man's strength,"[62] of what use is our notion of strength to Him, especially given our inclination to take credit for it? If God's power is always aligned with His purposes, why wouldn't He work through the part of us that is less inclined to resist Him and more inclined to rely on Him?

We are His people, and He is our God. When we submit our will to His will, His purposes become our purposes. We serve the poor on earth, and their praises reach the heavens. We proclaim the grace of the Christ now ascended and then marvel as His Spirit inhabits the hearts the humble. We stand in faith and prayer against the forces of evil and behold them flee before the God of all power.

He is well pleased to work His strength through our weakness. It all starts when we trust Him, loosen our grip on self-will, and give ourselves over to His ways.

God chose the weak things of the world to shame the strong. (1 Corinthians 1:27)

---

[62] 1 Corinthians 1:25

Strength to Stand

There was a time and place when, if you were born a Hatfield or a McCoy, you were born into a battle. Conflict was inevitable. It wasn't a matter of what you chose, but of who you were. We who are born into Christ join Him in battle, as well. His fight is not against countries, clans, or individuals, but against Satan and his underling spiritual forces of darkness. This "evil one" hates God and will use any means possible to deceive, tempt, accuse, and destroy God's people forever. We know this by experience, don't we?

With eternal consequences at stake, spiritual warfare demands spiritual strength. The problem is, on our own, we have none. "The spirit is willing," Jesus warned, "but the flesh is weak."[63] Knowing this, the apostle Paul provided basic instructions for spiritual conflict, a regimen every bit as effective for us today as when he wrote them in his letter to the Ephesian church:

We guard our minds with salvation as though it were a helmet,
And who is our salvation but Christ?

We fortify our hearts with righteousness as though it were a breastplate,
And who is our righteousness but Christ?

---

[63] Matthew 26:41 (NASB)

We secure ourselves in truth as though it were a belt,
And who is truth itself but Christ?

We equip our feet with the good news of peace,
And who is our peace but Christ?

We trust the Word of God as though it were a sword, piercing
to the truth of a matter,
And who is the Word of God but Christ?

We stand behind faith as though it were a shield against
all fear,
And in whom do we place our faith but Christ?

The armor we put on for strength *is* Christ! Nothing can overcome Him, for He is above "all rule and authority, power and dominion, and every title that can be given."[64] No wonder our enemy flees when we resist him! He looks at us and sees the all-powerful One who covers us from head to toe.

> *But the Lord is faithful, and he will strengthen and protect you from the evil one. (2 Thessalonians 3:3)*

---

[64] Ephesians 1:21, 22

The Power in Trust

When she was in high school, my daughter-in-law rowed on their Midwest champion crew. Not knowing a lot about the sport, I asked Gwen what quality was most crucial for team success. Was it strength? Technique? Timing? Her response surprised me. "Trust," she said, "Each person has to be able to trust in the commitment of everyone else in the boat." It makes sense. Whether we row together in the office, at church, in our marriage, or any other vessel in the flotilla, mistrust can slow us to a standstill, can't it? Associations fragment amid accusations. The greater "we" regresses into the lesser "me." Strength is sapped, and sync is sunk.

God loves unity. It is His own nature, and He created us to live in it. After all, what did God

"Trust," she said, "Each person has to be able to trust in the commitment of everyone else in the boat."

design marriage to be? The two become one. How did Jesus send out the seventy-two disciples? In pairs. What did Jesus pray for all who would believe in him? That we would be one with each other. What did He promise when two or more believers are gathered in His name? He'll be there; count on it. The "life boat" was built for team, and we glide faster when we row as one at the Coxswain's tempo.

We know people will let us down from time to time, however, so how do we commit ourselves to "everyone else in the boat"? Even when we're sailing smoothly in the moment, doubts linger, so how do we muster the discipline to propel well? We begin by anchoring our trust in God. He has a plan, a purpose, and a place for every believer, so we need not be distracted by our differences. He is powerfully at work in each member of the team, so we must not be fazed by others' flaws. He recruits new rowers, so we will not be overwhelmed at the oar. We are God's crew, and He knows what He is doing.

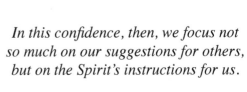

In this confidence, then, we focus not so much on our suggestions for others, but on the Spirit's instructions for us.

In this confidence, then, we focus not so much on our suggestions for others, but on the Spirit's instructions for us. We are not consumed by whether or not we can trust the team, rather we live in such a way as to gain their confidence. For when our sails are filled with the Spirit's wind, people gain strength from our support and take courage from our care. Their hope is harbored in harmony, and their power is preserved in peace.

Ultimately, our entire trust is in Christ who is at work in each of us to strengthen the team. In His power, we pull together, each committed to the other. This is the way of unity—the way of oneness—for "Christ is all, and is in all."[65]

[Love] always protects, always trusts, always hopes, always perseveres. (1 Corinthians 13:7)

---

[65] Colossians 3:11

Strength That Endures

A number of us had interviewed some candidates for a high-ranking position in the company and now gathered to share our observations. Of a particular applicant, one of my peers asked, "Does he have torque, or does he have horsepower?" I had never heard that juxtaposition in a leadership context before, but knew instantly what he meant. Torque gets us off to a quick start, but more important is horsepower, the sustainable strength needed for the long haul.

Our spiritual journey here is filled with joy and wonderment—we experience God in our own beings and witness His great works in and through the lives of others. Yet it also has its share of struggles and adversity; indeed, every day

But haven't we learned by now we can only run the engines of self-will at top speed for so long before they burn out?

we fight spiritual battles against powers far stronger than us. Temptations challenge us, rejections hurt us, and we share the pain of others along the way. We need strength for the journey, a certain kind of strength. We need horsepower. We need endurance.

Our tendency is to rely stoically on grit and determination. But haven't we learned by now we can only run the engines of self-will at top speed for so long before they burn out? The fact of the matter is, looking to our own reserves for spiritual strength is just one more temptation, one to which we too easily and often succumb—and so futilely! For as God speaks through the prophet, Jeremiah: "Cursed is the one who trusts in man, who depends on flesh for his strength and whose heart turns away from the Lord."[66]

As believers, we strain forward and press on toward our heavenly destination. Where do we find sustainable power for the journey? Isaiah steers us to its source, "those who hope in the Lord will renew their strength. They will soar on wings like eagles; they will run and not grow weary, they will walk and be not be faint."[67] The psalmist agrees: "Seek the Lord and his strength; seek his presence continually."[68]

It is in God himself we find our strength. He gives us quick-start torque when we need it, certainly, but horsepower for the long-haul, always.

> *Blessed are those whose strength is in you, who*
> *have set their hearts on pilgrimage . . . . They*
> *go from strength to strength, till each appears*
> *before God in Zion. (Psalm 84:5, 7)*

---

[66] Jeremiah 17:5
[67] Isaiah 40:31
[68] Psalm 105:4 (ESV)

8

Christ in Me Is Holiness

By nature, I am impure, but there is no impurity in Christ.
Christ is my life, and Christ in me is holiness.

The Face of Holiness

"**N**obody understands me." Have you ever heard someone say this? Have you ever said it yourself? Sometimes I think if "holiness" were to speak its thoughts, being misunderstood might be among them. We walk 360 degrees around holiness but never really "get" it. Occasionally, for instance, we utter the word in pejorative tones, such as when accusing others as being "holier than thou." And perhaps rightfully so because we also err in trying to *act* holy, as if we can *be* holy through religious posturing. Then there are times when, in an attempt to set ourselves apart from the *ways* of the world, we cut ourselves off from the *people* of the world. Finally, there's the "social relevance" question:

Holiness is not separating ourselves from the unjust people of the world, but from the unjust ways of the world.

of what value is an antiquated concept like holiness in a relativistic world where "it's all good" or a dysfunctional world in which bad is good and good is bad? Misunderstood, indeed!

So let's get a better glimpse of holiness. Let's put a face to it, the face of Jesus. He is, after all, the "exact representation" of God's being.[69] In the Sermon on the Mount, Jesus taught us what holiness looks like in action, what it means in a practical sense to devote ourselves wholly to God and His

---

[69] Hebrews 1:3

ways that we intuitively know are good and right. Living in holiness means we:

Forgive and resolve matters quickly, instead of holding grudges;

Take joy in our spouses and cherish our families, instead of looking elsewhere;

Seek good for those who hurt us, instead of perpetuating a cycle of retaliation;

Give, pray, and fast in secret, instead of showcasing our piety;

Trust God who loves us, instead of doubting His faithfulness;

Use our wealth for eternal good, instead of hoarding it for temporary comfort;

Attend to our own flaws, instead of presiding in judgment over the faults of others;

Treat others as we want to be treated, instead of letting their actions dictate ours; and

Share with others our reason for hope, instead of leaving them to search alone.

That's holiness! Practical holiness. That's what it looks like to launch from the gravitational pull of this world and to soar in the heavenly realms. Holiness is not separating ourselves from the unjust people of the world, but from the unjust ways of the world. It is not a matter of measuring our goodness against that of others, rather it is embracing with all our being the goodness of God.

"When Jesus had finished saying these things, the crowds were amazed at his teaching, because he taught as one who had authority, and not as their teachers of the law."[70] Whose heart doesn't leap at the voice of Truth and the call to live in His ways? There's nothing irrelevant about holiness. We crave it, actually.

You can readily recall, can't you, how at one time the more you did just what you felt like doing—not caring about others, not caring about God—the worse your life became and the less freedom you had? And how much different is it now as you live in God's freedom, your lives healed and expansive in holiness? (Romans 6:19 The Message)

---

[70] Matthew 7:28

Event and Process

As I write, our daughter-in-law, Gwen, is pregnant with Matthew's and her first child. She carries their daughter, and they will name her Abigail. It is a marvelous thing, this mother and her daughter in utero. Abigail shows quite a bit of independence, stirring and moving around whenever she wants to and resting when it best suits her. Night or day, Gwen really has no control over Abigail's little activity schedule. Still developing in the womb, however, Abigail remains completely dependent on her mother for safety, oxygen, nourishment, and all the essentials for life. She fully lives even as she continues to be formed.

Like a child kicking in the womb, holiness already lives and leaps in all who are in Christ. "We have been made holy," says the writer of Hebrews, "through the sacrifice of the body of Jesus Christ once for all."[71] For when this unblemished Lamb of God died for us, He took our impurities upon himself and buried them forever. Now risen from the dead, He breathes into all who trust in Him new life—His life—with divine DNA and its strands of holiness. As Christ is set apart unto God, so also are we who are in Christ set apart unto God. It is vital that we understand this element of our spiritual genetic make-up.

---

[71] Hebrews 10:10

If we have been cleansed of our corruption, why don't we feel like it, or for that matter, why don't we act like it? The writer went on to explain that being set apart unto God is also a process. While we have been "made perfect forever" by Christ in us, we are still "being made holy."[72] That is, we continue to be formed into the image of Christ, even as we fully live in Him. Our quest for gratification, then, gradually gives way to meaningful service to others. Greed is weeded from hearts now sprouting with generosity. Our souls begin to burn with more passion for God's will than for our own. The Spirit gently counsels, and we gladly listen. Inward emotions of love steadily mature into selfless acts of love. And our spirits pour forth praise to the One in whom we find life as it should be.

We cannot force our spiritual growth any more than Abigail can force her physical development, but we can yield our entire beings to the Spirit's work in us. For we are holy lives being made holy.

But now he has reconciled you by Christ's
physical body through death to present you
holy in his sight, without blemish and free
from accusation—if you continue in your faith,
established and firm, not moved from the hope
held out in the gospel. (Colossians 1:22, 23)

---

[72] Hebrews 10:14

117

Be Holy

There comes a time when a young woman studying dance is made the company's lead ballerina, even as she daily perfects her pirouette en pointe. There comes a point at which a young man tossing the football is named the team's starting quarterback, even as he continues to develop his five-step drop. Both have become what they aspired to be, even as they refine what they have become. For each of them, however, one thing remains: he must take the field, and she must take the stage. Until they do, they contribute little more than their names in the program.

Christ has removed our impurities and reunited us with God, even as the Holy Spirit continues to hone our holiness. So like the dancer and the athlete, one thing for us remains: we must go out and be holy, for being separated from the ways of the world and unto God has empowering purpose. Whatever our venue, we step into it "made holy, useful to the Master and prepared to do any good work."[73]

When patrons attend the ballet, they put their cares behind them for an evening of beauty and grace. As the fans fill the stands, all else is forgotten; they are there to cheer excellence and triumph. Now, surely no one makes plans to go see people devoted to God, but they do pay attention, hoping to find a better way in life, for deep inside, people desire:

---

[73] 2 Timothy 2:21

to leave futility behind and find meaning;
to leave scorn behind and find worth;
to leave ostracism behind and find embrace;
to leave inauthenticity behind and find real;
to leave isolation behind and find engagement;
to leave apathy behind and find care;
to leave judgment behind and find mercy;
to leave criticism behind and find encouragement;
to leave grudges behind and find forgiveness;
to leave uncertainty behind and find bedrock;
to leave apprehension behind and find trust; and
to leave unbelief behind and find life.

Although they may not articulate it this way, people yearn to leave behind the oppressive ways of the world and to experience the pure ways of God. So, in love for all, God says to his people:

Be holy, because I, the Lord your God, am holy. (Leviticus 19:2)

The New Clothes of Freedom

I ndulge me for a moment. Imagine today is the day you are released from prison. You've counted down to this moment ever since the high-pitched gavel of judgment echoed your guilt throughout the courtroom. You've served the sentence for your wrong, and now the authorities say you're free. Ahead of you lies the hope of a life the way it was meant to be lived. It is time to go.

Of all the decisions before you, the first one is profoundly simple and clear: You set aside your state-issued uniform and dress now in the civilian clothes of freedom. Whether you've done your time in prison blues, jailhouse orange, or horizontal stripes, they are now in your past. You are no longer forced to wear them, and you most assuredly don't want to. There is no use in clinging to them any longer. While you will always remember the lessons learned from your time in captivity, your new life of liberty will not resemble it, nor will your attire. No, the time has come to "put off" the old and to "put on" the new.

The Bible teaches us that all who are born into Christ Jesus have been liberated from a far greater sentence, an eternal separation from God. In fact, Jesus came for this purpose, to release us from condemnation.[74] Guiding our transition into the free world, then, Paul offers this pressing

---

[74] John 3:17

reminder: "You were taught, with regard to your former way of life, to put off your old self, which is being corrupted by its deceitful desires; to be made new in the attitude of your minds; and to put on the new self, created to be like God in true righteousness and holiness."[75] Just as those released from physical captivity set aside their old uniforms, we who have been freed from spiritual lock-up leave behind our "old self" with its patterns of pride, greed, lust, and all outward expressions of its inward nature.

Note that we are not called to alter our sin nature into something more acceptable to God, as though we can sanctify ourselves through behavior modification. We cannot. Likewise, we do not launder our old self by our own attempts to be righteous or holy, for even our greatest attempts to do so result in "filthy rags."[76] No, we simply set aside that which cannot be improved; we "put off" the old self, for it defines us no longer. And we "put on" our new self, which is tailored in the image of Christ. All of us who were baptized into Christ have "clothed"[77] ourselves with Him, says Paul. Moreover, we are woven into Christ, for we live in Him and He in us.

Therefore, we venture into the world full of challenges, both external and within. Make no mistake—we will be tempted to break out the old prison garb of the soul and confront opposition on our own terms, our old terms. But we are

---

[75] Ephesians 4:22—24
[76] Isaiah 64:6
[77] Galatians 3:27

free people now, and so Paul appeals to us instead: "clothe yourselves with the Lord Jesus Christ, and do not think about how to gratify the desires of the sinful nature."[78]

Jesus has made us holy, even as He continues to do so. He has commissioned us to go out and be holy. So we break the bond of recidivism, for no longer is our identity reduced to a number proclaiming our oppression; rather, we put on Christ, and we bear the name of Him who is holy by nature.

---

[78] Romans 13:14

9

Christ in Me Is Wisdom

By nature, I am foolish, but there is no foolishness in Christ.
Christ is my life, and Christ in me is wisdom.

Precious or Faux?

I know a dear woman who wears on her hand a five-carat diamond, set in titanium. She doesn't hide it away or bring it out only for special occasions; she enjoys it every day. I don't know how much the gem is worth. I never asked. Let's just say—a lot. Diamonds have intrinsic value, and a five-carat one has more than most!

The Scriptures tell us wisdom—knowing God and living according to His ways—is of greater value than gold, silver, and precious gems[79] and that it is better to obtain wisdom and understanding than any treasures.[80] For what metal or mineral can protect us and watch over us as wisdom does?[81] What can we drape around our neck or slide onto our finger to gain understanding and discretion, well-being and honor, counsel and justice?[82]

At the time of this writing, a five-carat cubic zirconia is easily available on-line for $39.00. Compared to "the real thing," this piece of imitation jewelry has very little inherent value; its worth is determined only by how much we are willing to pay for something that looks like something it isn't! Similarly, there are plenty of faux wisdom replicas in the world, all of them formed without the precious component of

---

[79] Proverbs 3:13–15
[80] Proverbs 16:16
[81] Proverbs 4:6
[82] Proverbs 8:12–21

God's truth. Such human wisdom appears real, but its value is limited. As the prophet, Jeremiah, rhetorically laments, "Since they have rejected the word of the Lord, what kind of wisdom do they have?"[83] After all, how insightful can we be without the understanding of God who brought forth wisdom "as the first of his works"?[84] What can the "wisdom of the world" be worth if it is not set in the certainty of who God is and the ways He has decreed?

Solomon advised, "Wisdom is supreme; therefore get wisdom. Though it cost all you have, get understanding."[85] He spoke not of human wisdom, the costume jewelry of our nature, but of wisdom from God—the clarity of His truth, the brilliance of His being, the adornment of our spirits.

The foolishness of God is wiser than man's wisdom. (1 Corinthians 1:25)

---

[83] Jeremiah 8:9
[84] Proverbs 8:22
[85] Proverbs 4:7

The Rendezvous Point

Have you ever frantically searched for a child who was frantically searching for you? Or was it you, the lost child looking for a parent? Perhaps it was in the woods or at Disney World or in the mall. Wherever its locale at any given moment, "lost" is a very distressing place to be!

People all over the world search for wisdom; we share an inner longing for true knowledge, understanding, and insight. We seek the inner compass that navigates us from naiveté to discernment, from recklessness to discretion, from injustice to fairness, from discord to peace. We pursue meaning that we know exists in an authority outside of ourselves, elusive though it seems, beyond our natural reach.

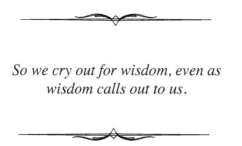

So we cry out for wisdom, even as wisdom calls out to us.

The quest for wisdom transcends generational boundaries, and Solomon, regarded the wisest man who ever lived, promised this to all of us who embark upon it: if we "call out for insight and cry aloud for understanding,"[86] we will discover it. If we "look for it as for silver and search for it as for hidden treasure," then we will find "the knowledge of God."[87] If this

---

[86] Proverbs 2:3
[87] Proverbs 2:4, 5

127

weren't encouraging enough, the ancient king of Israel assured us wisdom is looking for us, too! "Does not wisdom call out? Does not understanding raise her voice? . . . 'To you, O men, I call out; I raise my voice to all mankind. You who are simple, gain prudence; you who are foolish, gain understanding.'"[88]

So we cry out for wisdom, even as wisdom calls out to us. To our great relief, there is a rendezvous point, a place where we would-be companions can find each other. It is the spot on the map marked, "the fear of the Lord." It is the point at which we believe God, trust God, relinquish our wills to His ways, and rest our weary souls in Him. Those who seek insight can be united with it there, for "The fear of the Lord is the beginning of wisdom, and knowledge of the Holy One is understanding."[89]

Go to that spot—the place of reverence for God and awe of Him, the place of belief and trust in His Word. There you will find wisdom waiting for you.

If any of you lacks wisdom, let him ask God,
who gives generously to all without reproach,
and it will be given him. (James 1:5 ESV)

---

[88] Proverbs 8:1, 4, 5
[89] Proverbs 9:10

Creed and Deed

Are you familiar with the "knowing-doing gap"? It is a common phenomenon in which people *talk* about an issue, perhaps *learn* a lot about it, but don't *do* anything about it. Many meetings close with participants somehow thinking that, by discussing an issue, they've actually done something to address it, even though their contemplations never even approached a resolution, let alone an action step!

Wisdom has no knowing-doing gap. *Knowing* what is best and not *doing* what is best is really pretty silly. "Foolish," we might say. It's the opposite of wisdom. Solomon knew this. When God told the king in a dream to ask for whatever he wanted, Solomon

Wisdom is both creed and deed; it is acting on what we know to be true.

requested "a discerning heart,"[90] for he needed understanding and insight to distinguish between right and wrong as he governed Israel. Wisdom to Solomon was for a purpose beyond mere knowledge; he knew understanding as something to be applied.

Jesus knew it, too. His Sermon on the Mount was wisdom from God concerning forgiveness, enemies, fidelity,

---

[90] 1 Kings 3:9

possessions, judgment, faith, and several other life challenges. Then concluding his instruction, He specifically cautioned against any knowing-doing gap: "Therefore everyone who hears these words of mine and puts them into practice is like a wise man who built his house on the rock. . . . But everyone who hears these words of mine and does not put them into practice is like a foolish man who built his house on sand."[91]

Wisdom is both creed and deed; it is acting on what we know to be true. In fact, the apostle James said that if we hear the word and don't do the word, it eludes us. If, on the other hand, we apply what we come to know, we are blessed.[92] His simple advice? "Do not merely listen to the word, and so deceive yourselves. Do what it says."[93]

> *Who is wise and understanding among you?*
> *Let him show it by his good life, by deeds*
> *done in the humility that comes from wisdom.*
> *(James 3:13)*

---

[91] Matthew 7:24, 26
[92] James 1:23–25
[93] James 1:22

A Tool for Any Job

Just before Peggy and I were married, her parents surprised me with a large, durable, metal tool box. Inside, it was thoughtfully filled with a wide assortment of tools, each, of course, with its own purpose. It was so fun to open this "gift that kept giving"—to unpack it item by item and appreciate every practical tool it contained. Through the years, I've used every one of them many times.

For ages, God had also kept hidden a present for His people until just the right time to reveal it. Oh, He hinted at it often enough through His prophets. Jeremiah, for instance, foretold that we would know God, and Ezekiel spoke of a day when the Spirit would live in us and move us in His ways. But no one could figure out the mystery, no matter how they shook the package or peeked through its paper. For God's was an unimaginable gift—His Son living in us, His Spirit breathing never-ending life into each person who receives Him.

This Christ is also a gift that keeps giving; there is much more to Him than we initially realize. He is holy, and He becomes our holiness. He is righteous, and He credits His righteousness to us. He is our peace; in Him our souls find rest. He who holds all power is strength to us. And among all the surprises in the box lies one particularly practical one, for in Christ also are hidden "all the treasures of wisdom and knowledge."[94] Understanding is no longer "out there" somewhere; it resides in Christ, and Christ resides in us! Contemplate this; absorb it. It's a promise; it is true.

Wisdom is a versatile tool we can apply in any number of situations. With Christ in us and His insights held firmly in our grasp, we can open the flow of justice around us, measure our speech in truthful and loving terms, balance our financial stewardship, and detect the ways that are good and right. In Christ, we can cut off any notion of infidelity, smooth the rough edges of indiscretion, and guard our health and safety. In Him, we can tighten the bonds of friendship and "chisel away" at any inclination to embrace what we know to be wrong.

Understanding God and living in His ways do not come naturally to us. It takes time, patience, and learning—a renewing of the mind—to grasp His truth and apply it skillfully in our lives. But the Spirit of Christ is always with us, always in us, and reminding us of everything we've learned from Jesus, the master craftsman from Nazareth.

Let the word of Christ dwell in you richly, teaching and admonishing one another in all wisdom. (Colossians 3:16 ESV)

---

[94] Colossians 2:3

10

Christ in Me Is Humility

By nature, I am prideful, but there is no pridefulness in Christ. Christ is my life, and Christ in me is humility.

Humility—Emptied of Pride

> *When Simon Peter saw this, he fell at Jesus'*
> *knees and said, "Go away from me, Lord; I*
> *am a sinful man!" (Luke 5:8)*

I t was a humbling moment for Peter and every bit as revealing. Jesus the carpenter had told this fisherman by trade where to cast his nets. Though discouraged from his own fruitless toil, and presuming to know better, Peter reluctantly obliged, perhaps out of respect for the man. When his nets filled to the point of breaking and the boats to the point of sinking, however, Peter fell to his knees, not from the weight of the catch, but at a clearer glimpse of himself in the light of Christ. Humbled in the moment, Peter's wounded pride yet lay bare before the Son of God. Go away! Just go away!

Isn't it odd the more closely we experience God, the more we realize how far apart we are in the first place?

Isn't it odd the more closely we experience God, the more we realize how far apart we are in the first place? The disparities between our sin nature and His divine nature shouldn't surprise us, though, for God declared through His prophet Isaiah, "As the heavens are higher than the earth, so are my ways higher than your ways and my thoughts than your thoughts."[95] Perhaps no contrast is as stark as that between the pride of a sinful people and the humility of a holy God.

Pride compels us to a fool's errand: to close this distance from the Divine on our own terms. Like the builders of Babel, we erect towers in our hearts and ascend them to God's place as the lord and judge over the world around us. Were we ever to reach the heavens, however, we might be surprised to find a humble God stooping low toward the earth to serve and to save a confused and helpless people. Though we rise up and assert ourselves against Him, He descends in compassion to a people tangled up in a pride that so ironically betrays our own flaws.

Isn't it telling, for instance, we vindicate ourselves before God and people by pointing to the shortcomings of others? If we are truly convinced of our greatness, why must we constantly prove it, even to ourselves, by parading our possessions and posturing our positions? If life is all about us, why do we always feel best when we've done something for others, and where does that warm glow come from, anyway? What do we reveal about ourselves when we don the mask of false humility? How harsh the life that serves one's pride! How mercilessly it mocks us in return!

---

[95] Isaiah 55:9

Yet God loves us. In grace, He convicts us. He waits for us, watches over us and even serves us until the day when we come to the end of ourselves and leave behind our old nets filled only with empty pride. This is the way of Christ . . .

Who, being in very nature God, did not consider equality with God something to be grasped, but made himself nothing, taking the very nature of a servant, being made in human likeness. And being found in appearance as a man, he humbled himself and became obedient to death—even death on a cross! (Philippians 2:6–8)

Humility—Filled with Christ

Then Jesus said to Simon, "Don't be afraid;
from now on you will catch men." So they
pulled their boats up on shore, left everything
and followed him. (Luke 5:10, 11)

I t is a curious grace to reach the empty end of ourselves. Like frustrated fishermen, we have cast enormous nets for our own glory only to be disappointed with our catch. Whether we've hauled in knowledge or wealth, fame or stature, advancement or achievement, none have measured up to our expectations. Dissatisfied, we drop our nets again and again in search for more and more until we realize and confess the futility and mockery of "it's all about me." In these precious times of truth so convicting, we relinquish our pride so unfulfilling. Yet what God empties He also fills. We are thus twice-humbled: deservedly brought low in the pride of our sinful nature, then graciously raised up as partakers in Christ's divine nature. Is it any wonder, when called to follow Jesus, Peter and his friends left it all behind to follow Him? Doesn't His love compel us to do the same?

Then how amazing the things are that God does through people who are humbled in their flesh and living boldly in the humility of Christ! Who but hearts awakened by grace rise to seek and to serve those they once distanced in indifference or contempt? Who releases grudges held against others but those who sigh in relief over their own forgiveness? Who speaks as ambassadors of the Kingdom of God but those He has liberated from fear? Who stands in prayer against the powers of darkness but the one who has overcome them in Christ? And only in the love and power of Christ's sacrifice for us do we gratefully offer our life to Him.

"Humble yourselves, therefore, under God's mighty hand, that he may lift you up in due time,"[96] wrote the older, wiser Peter. Humility is the nature of Christ, and when we examine ourselves in the light of One so great, we cannot help but give Him all glory, for it is rightfully His.

> *Therefore God exalted him to the highest place and gave him the name that is above every name, that at the name of Jesus every knee should bow, in heaven and on earth and under the earth, and every tongue confess that Jesus Christ is Lord, to the glory of God the Father. (Philippians 2:9–11)*

---

[96] 1 Peter 5:6

Running First, Running Last

My niece was an outstanding high-school track athlete, clearly the best in her school at her events and quite frequently winning in area competition. In practice one day, Meghan eased off the throttle a bit (we all have those days), and one of her teammates outran her. Seeing this and knowing Meghan's ability, the coach challenged her with a great piece of competitive advice, "If you're going to be number one, you must always be number one. In a race or in practice, you must always win." Although mental toughness was one of Meghan's greatest strengths, this was needed counsel for champions.

Perhaps unknowingly, Meghan's coach had echoed an analogy the apostle Paul used to urge on the early church: "Do you not know that in a race all the runners run, but only one gets the prize? Run in such a way as to get the prize. Everyone who competes in the games goes into strict training. They do it to get a crown that will not last; but we do it to get a crown that will last forever."[97]

In the Kingdom of God, however, winning looks a little different than in this world. OK, a lot different! "If anyone wants to be first," Jesus told those closest to Him, "he must be the very last, and the servant of all."[98] In the Kingdom, "everybody else" matters as much as each one of us, and

---

[97] 1 Corinthians 9:24, 25
[98] Mark 9:35

serving others is more glorious than existing to be served. Were He to see us flagging in humility, Jesus might pull us aside with this piece of coaching advice, "If you're going to be number one, you must always be *last*. In a race or in practice, you must always be *last*."

When we live life in the humility of Christ, we hold others only in highest esteem. If God made everything from the wondrously complex cell to the unfathomable universe and yet formed only people into His image, how great must each person be? If God himself took on human form to become a sacrifice for us, then how can we even begin to know the value of each soul? If every time we feed the hungry, clothe those in need, or visit the sick or imprisoned, we do so also to Jesus, what must we conclude about His heart toward those we too often marginalize? We are surrounded by priceless people.

Then what's not to savor about humility? What's not to embrace? Humility is not something to which we merely acquiesce; it is a blessing in which we are privileged to partake. It is the lens through which we see people for who they are—God's greatest treasures—and care for them accordingly.

So we run with royalty. As we warm up for today's race, let us first rid the track of our hurdles of personal pride. Then when the gun sounds and the runners take off, let's drop back to run with the Leader and to celebrate what we've missed all this time from our normal "me first" position, namely the miracle of everyone else.

Love one another with brotherly affection. Outdo one another in showing honor. (Romans 12:10 ESV)

When Knowledge Grows Up

A ll children dream of what they want to be when they grow up. Take young Knowledge, for instance: When Knowledge grows up, he wants to be a doer. After all, he has had a good role model:

Knowledge is not the end in itself; rather, it must mature into love, trust in God, and obey in acts of service.

It was just before the Passover Feast. Jesus knew that the time had come for him to leave this world and go to the Father. Having loved his own who were in the world, he now showed them the full extent of his love. The evening meal was being served . . . Jesus knew that the Father had put all things under his power, and that he had come from God and was returning to God; so he got up from the meal, took off his outer clothing and wrapped a towel around his waist. After that, he poured water into a basin and began to wash his disciples' feet.[99]

Think of all that Jesus knew about His last week on earth. He knew Judas would betray Him. He knew Peter would deny

---

[99] John 13:1–5

Him. He knew the Jews would condemn Him. He knew the Gentiles would mock Him, insult Him, spit on Him, flog Him, and crucify Him. The Scriptures had foretold all of this, and Jesus knew the Scriptures. So knowing his time had come, what did Jesus do? He got up from the meal and assumed a lowly servant's task—He washed His disciples' feet. Pride could not constrain Him, for He had nothing to prove! He knew who He was, and He knew whom He loved; He was free to serve others.

It was an object lesson for the ages: Knowledge is not the end in itself; rather, it must mature into love, trust in God, and obey in acts of service. Jesus concluded with this brief commencement address, which was recorded for remote learners in all the years to come: "You call me 'Teacher' and 'Lord,' and rightly so, for that is what I am. Now that I, your Lord and Teacher, have washed your feet, you also should wash one another's feet. . . . Now that you *know* these things, you will be blessed if you *do* them."[100]

In most of us, Knowledge has learned enough from the Teacher to go and serve others in the name of its Lord. To some, we bring encouragement. To some, we bring food. To some, we speak wisdom into confusion. To some, we simply listen, and to all, we bring truth and life in Jesus' name.

So we emerge from our Bible studies and venture forth into the world around us. We have absorbed much at the

---

[100]John 13:13, 14, 17

tranquil school of learning, and it is time to go to work and apply our knowledge, no matter how humble the task.

Knowledge puffs up, but loves builds up.
(1 Corinthians 8:1)

11

Christ in Me Is Hope

By nature, I am despairing,
but there is no despair in Christ.
Christ is my life, and Christ in me is hope.

Our Hope for Forgiveness

> *Son of man, say to the house of Israel, "This*
> *is what you are saying: 'Our offenses and*
> *sins weigh us down, and we are wasting away*
> *because of them. How then can we live?'"*
> *(Ezekiel 33:10)*

S ound familiar? Do you ever feel as though you're "wasting away" under the weight of guilt? If so, you're in some pretty good company. With refreshing candor, King David penned to verse, "I know my transgressions, and my sin is always before me."[101] Opening himself like a book before generations to come, Paul likewise lamented, "What a wretched man I am! Who will rescue me from this body of death?"[102]

Were we to be so honest, we would all have to concede guilt is simply too much for any of us to handle. It's not

The problem of sin, so much bigger than us, demands a hope so much bigger than us.

for a lack of trying; on the contrary, we've tried everything! We've denied our wrong, blamed our neighbors, and wrung our hands, but our sins still cling to us like those pesky foam

---

[101]Psalm 51:3
[102]Romans 7:24

packing peanuts! Are we compensating by doing good or pretending by acting good? They're distractions at best. Are we resolving to do better? By now, we know better!

We can remain there, struggling alone in our natural limitations if we wish, hopeless and helpless against guilt. But like the rich young ruler, unwilling to choose God over riches and unable to atone for it, we eventually turn around in sadness and walk away from God.[103] In this way, perhaps it is true that "Despair is a greater sin than any of the sins that provoke it,"[104] as C. S. Lewis once wrote. Yet it need not be this way. Not at all!

The problem of sin, so much bigger than us, demands a hope so much bigger than us. God has given us such a hope! God, himself, *is* our hope. The sacrifice of the crucified Christ expunged our guilt for all time. The Spirit of the risen Christ is life in us forever.

We don't need to waste away under our sins; we can live lives freed from the weight of them.

We don't need to conceal our offenses; we can confess openly to God who already knows them.

We don't need to strive for atonement; we can trust Christ who has reunited us with God.

We don't need to run away from God in fear; we can run to Him in confidence.

---

[103]Matthew 19:21, 22
[104]C. S. Lewis, The Screwtape Letters, (New York: Harper Collins), 162.

150

We don't need to be absorbed in our guilt; we are free to care for others.

We don't need to look down in shame; we can look up to God in gratitude.

We don't need to despair in our helplessness; our hope is well founded in Christ.

> *Praise be to the God and Father of our Lord Jesus Christ! In his great mercy he has given us new birth into a living hope through the resurrection of Jesus Christ from the dead. (1 Peter 1:3)*

Hope amid Rejection and Pain

I had been removed from a position at work, from a division I had led, and a people I had loved. It hurt me deeply and shook me to the core. Had I been perfect? No. Did I deserve this? No, not in my estimation, anyway. The decision had been made, however, and I found myself struggling with a deep sense of injustice. Although I had observed it plenty throughout the years, I had not lived as one reeling from the feeling of wrong.

And *I* had landed on my feet! I was still employed by the company, still well compensated, and now in

Hope—it is the confident expectation of good, regardless of circumstance.

a new position with a new challenge to embrace. So if my world was so rocked and racked with pain, I had no choice but to muse about those who *really* knew injustice, such as people profiled by outward appearance, the naïve innocents manipulated and coerced into sex trafficking, lives lived behind bars for something they did not do, and the child beaten by the parent whose love he craves, confused and wondering, "Why? What did I do?"

Despair—it's where we find ourselves when we are utterly at a loss. It is that place where we are overwhelmed by things that aren't as they should be, where we are overcome by wrongs too big for us to right. So we live there in despair, some of us only temporarily and some of us not so fortunate.

Sometime before I sensed any change at work—before I realized that things might not go well for me—God had pulled me close to Him. I had begun to read His Word daily and to journal what it was teaching me and how it was changing me. It wasn't long before I began to grasp how personal God's love was for me, that He was even more eager than I to spend time together. I began to "get" David, the psalmist, and his complete openness before God. I began to "get" John, the apostle in awe of Jesus' love for him. The Spirit of God was changing me through the Word of God, and I lived daily in hope.

Hope—it is the confident expectation of good, regardless of circumstance. When my rejection and pain came at work, I knew this hope. I had experienced it. It was mine. So even as this difficult season had now come upon me, God continued to open my eyes to His truths, assuring me of His presence and filling me with His joy. Each day, I expected good and, every morning, He who is goodness fulfilled my hope. His presence with me—His Word and His Spirit in me—*was* my hope.

So I found myself knowing an unimaginable joy while suffering an unprecedented pain. For God did not walk me around the crucible; we walked right through its purifying heat together—joy triumphing over pain and hope defeating despair.

May the God of hope fill you with all joy and peace as you trust in him, so that you may overflow with hope by the power of the Holy Spirit. (Romans 15:13)

Our Hope in the Circumstances of Life

When our son, Matthew, was a boy, we would occasionally tell him, "When life gets tough, know that there is always a better day coming." We would have this little conversation during good times to stock him up with a ready source and supply of hope for when things turned difficult. Amid the wonderful laughter, warmth, and joys of life arise its difficult moments, days, and seasons. They may be rooted in hurts from others or the wrongs of our own making, but hardships just as readily arise out of the circumstances of everyday life in a broken-down world.

Tough times are unavoidable in the human experience, and they hurt! We lose people we have loved, or we watch helplessly as their health declines toward what will come. We stagger under unreasonable workloads, made heavier by unrealistic timeframes. Our investments are walloped by volatile markets, our possessions consumed by unforeseen calamities. We are caught up in lay-offs at the hand of those who measure their leadership by our engagement. Even Jesus agonized in Gethsemane, "My soul is overwhelmed with sorrow to the point of death."[105] Of their sufferings, Paul and Timothy wrote, "We were under great pressure, far beyond our ability to endure, so that we despaired even of life."[106] No one is exempt from troubles; none of us escape.

Yet difficulties always lead us to a fork in the road and an unavoidable decision between two very different paths. One

---

[105]Matthew 26:38
[106]2 Corinthians 1:8

way is called Hope. It rises to a place where the fogs of circumstance, no matter how thick, cease to cloud our sight. The goodness that surrounds us breaks through, no longer obscured; we look up and see joy. When the journey becomes challenging, we remain firmly footed on the way of Hope, itself a reliable companion.

How different, this way of Hope from the other path named Despair! Despair is an overwhelming struggle; we trudge its trail bent low and bowed down by its overgrowth of worries and cares. As we plod along this lonely path of our choosing, Despair diverges ever farther into isolation, to the point at which Hope fades from view. Eventually, we doubt it exists.

So how do we choose the way of Hope? First, be honest. Life's circumstances can easily overpower our ability to overcome them on our own, and the sooner we admit this to ourselves, the better. Second, trust that God is greater than our circumstances. Think back on past difficulties and reflect on God's presence throughout them, which is always clearer when viewed through the lens of hindsight. Then in that hope, trust He will see you through the struggles you face now and those you will face in the future, for He is faithful.

Christ goes with us and in us, for He himself is our way of Hope. Our reliable companion.

Why are you in despair, O my soul? And why have you become disturbed within me? Hope in God, for I shall again praise him for the help of his presence. (Psalm 42:5 NASB)

Our Hope of Glory

My father was a good dad. As a young boy, I loved him, admired him, and trusted him. At age seven, I also lost him—he died of a heart attack one summer Sunday morning. Though there were plenty of happy moments in the growing-up years that followed, they emerged against a backdrop of emptiness and loss. My father was gone, and a great deal of my childlike trust in God might as well have been buried with him.

For our hope is not the human notion of mere possibility or even optimism; our hope is the certainty of Christ.

Years later when I was a young man, I had a dream. In my dream, my father was with me again, and I was bringing him up to date on what had happened in my life—that I had gone to college, graduated, and launched my career. His attention was undivided as he listened with interest, pride, and affirmation. So when I went on to tell him also about my brother's and sister's lives, he said in warmth and kindness, "I know. You don't have to tell me." A bit confused, I paused and said, "I just wanted you to know what else has happened in our family since you died." Then with an assuring grin and his peaceful blue eyes, he replied simply, "I never died." I immediately awoke with tears as warm as my father's love and a heart daring to hope again in our God and His promise of eternal life.

There's a whole lot we won't know about the next life until we get there. No eye has seen it, no ear has heard it, and no mind has conceived it.[107] But we do know this—life will be as we know down deep it is supposed to be. There will be no more mourning, for there will be no more death. There will be no more crying, for there will be no more pain. There will be no more heartache, for God will wipe every tear from our eyes.[108]

We will finally realize just how much God loves us and how highly He treasures us. We will discover the magnificence in which He created us and to which He has already begun to restore us. For though we fall far short of His splendor, He is already at work, transforming us "into his likeness with ever-increasing glory, which comes from the Lord, who is the Spirit."[109] Yes, we will again know the glory our loving God intended for us from the beginning, and in this hope we rejoice. For our hope is not the human notion of mere possibility or even optimism; our hope is the certainty of Christ. He who has fulfilled the promises of ages past lives today as our hope for an eternity of glorious

---

[107] 1 Corinthians 2:9
[108] Revelation 21:4
[109] 2 Corinthians 3:18

tomorrows. He is our hope. He is "Christ in you, the hope of glory."[110]

> When Christ, who is your life, appears, then you also will appear with him in glory. *(Colossians 3:4)*

---

[110]Colossians 1:27

12

Christ in Me Is Life

By nature, I am dying, but there is no death in Christ.
Christ is my life, forever.

Do You Believe This?

"They don't have a chance." It's what we project for those attempting the impossible while facing the inevitable. We admire their efforts and affirm their optimism in whatever their endeavor, but we pretty much know their eventual outcome. It can be said, for instance, of our innate ability—or, better yet, inability—to live forever. Though people throughout the ages have yearned to drink from an elusive fountain of youth, we haven't possessed the means. Death is, they say, as certain as taxes!

It wasn't meant to be this way. God created us to be body and spirit, our body from the dust of the ground and our spirit from His breath of life. His deep desire—indeed, His original design—was for us to live in a world that is all we know it should be, a creation in which everything is good and, altogether, very good. God protectively urged Adam to live and thrive safely inside this Paradise, saying, "You must not eat from the tree of the knowledge of good and evil, for when you eat of it you will surely die."[111] Adam disobeyed, of course, so we all face a certain but unknowable date when our dust returns to dust, our bodies to the ground.

So then what? Down deep, we all know—and most of us will admit—that something lies beyond the here and now, but what do we do about it? We will all be buried, but who can rise? If we can't even keep ourselves from dying, how

[111] Genesis 2:17

do we pull off an afterlife? Even if we do rise again to life, how can we, who cannot keep from sinning for a single day, live before a holy God who wisely does not compromise His purity? Nowhere are the limitations of our sinful selves so apparent than when contemplating our sure demise.

But the power of God transcends our weakness, the love of God outmuscles our fear, and the God of life consumes our death. How can this be? Jesus has made us one with Him; our spirit lives in Him as His Spirit lives in us. As the apostle Paul explained, our lives are "hidden with Christ in God,"[112] and therein lies the miracle of life that never ends. For this Christ suffered for us the death our sins deserved; yet, being sinless Himself, He rose again to life. Since our lives are "hidden" in Christ, we died with Him; His death was our death. And because Jesus lives in all who believe Him; His resurrection to life is our resurrection, too! Paul put it this way: "If we have been united with him like this in his death, we will certainly also be united with him in his resurrection."[113]

Our eternal life, then, is God himself living in us, Jesus the Anointed One. He once said to Martha, a friend and follower of His, "I am the resurrection and the life. He who believes in me will live, even though he dies; and whoever lives and believes in me will never die. Do you believe this?"[114] Martha answered, "Yes." So can we—and live.

---

[112]Colossians 3:3
[113]Romans 6:5
[114]John 11:25, 26

Faith beyond Belief!

A man once said to me, "I have a hard time accepting the idea that God will only let me into heaven if I believe a certain thing or a certain way. So I live my entire life and, at the end, it all comes down to whether or not I believe something to be true? I've seen big changes in my friends and family members who believe, so I want to believe, but I have a hard time accepting this." The man's openness was refreshing, and I completely understood his skepticism. For if belief is nothing more than admitting the truth of a matter, I think he has a point. Mere acknowledgment of fact, how-

Taking this cross-over step of faith, we emerge from the shadows of our hiding and enter into restored relationship with God.

ever sincere, is something less than transformational. The apostle James gave voice to the sentiment this way: "You believe that there is one God. Good! Even the demons believe that—and shudder."[115]

Biblical belief is so much richer, so much warmer, and so much more substantial than an academic nod of agreement from afar. For the foundation of our faith is so much more than a mere notion or idea; He is Jesus Christ, the Son of God, in whom life exists. Jesus assures us, "as the Father has life in

---

[115]James 2:19

165

himself, so he has granted the Son to have life in himself."[116] So also the apostle Paul attests of Christ, "All things were created through him and for him," he writes, ". . . he is before all things, and in him all things hold together."[117] The belief to which God calls us, then, far surpasses mental assent; He invites us to a place called faith, where we entrust our very lives to Him in whom eternity exists. "I tell you the truth," Jesus said, "whoever hears my word and believes him who sent me has eternal life and will not be condemned; he has crossed over from death to life."[118]

Taking this cross-over step of faith, we emerge from the shadows of our hiding and enter into restored relationship with God. We experience Him as He transforms us, and we enjoy Him, for He is not a belief system of our making, but the abundant life of our longing.

If the Spirit is stirring in you to be reconciled to God through His Son, you can respond by praying:

> Jesus, I know I cannot gain eternal life on my own or by my own merit. I do not live as you would have me live. For this I am very sorry. I believe you are the Son of God and that you paid the penalty for my sins because you love me. I believe you rose again to never-ending

---

[116] John 5:26
[117] Colossians 1:16, 17 (ESV)
[118] John 5:24

life and that you offer that life to me as a gift. I entrust myself to you, receive your gift now, and by your promise, cross over from death to life. Fill me with your Spirit and use me for your honor and glory. Thank you for your precious gift of life in me.

I write these things to you who believe in the name of the Son of God so that you may know that you have eternal life. (1 John 5:13)

We Will Be Changed

H ave you ever held garden seeds in your hand? How would you describe them? Small? Earth tone? Irregular? Although amazingly complex, there is nothing about them that catches the eye; in fact, unless they are bunched together, we walk past them without a notice. If only we could see their potential, though, what they would become. The apostle Paul said our earthly bodies are like these seeds in a way: though we are wonderfully made, we weaken and die. We return to the earth, each one of us. Yet this is not the end of the story; it's not our final act.

Instead, we live and die boldly—living in the assurance of eternity and dying in the confidence of change. Though our bodies are "sown" like seeds that fall to the ground, we will yet rise up with spiritual bodies in an imperishable glory given to us by God. We will bear the likeness of Christ, who has already risen from death, as witnessed by many.

How do we know the glory that awaits us? Simply this: God always does what He says he will do. To Abraham He promised a blessing and a seed, both ultimately fulfilled in the person of Jesus Christ. To Moses He promised to call forth another prophet like Him, a promise also kept in Christ. To David, He promised a descendant as king forever, again fulfilled in this Son of God. Through the prophets, God foretold so many things about the Messiah—details about His birth, His life, His death, and His resurrection—all of these promises kept in Jesus the Christ.

And now through Paul, God promises again: we will rise. "The Lord Jesus Christ," penned the apostle, ". . . will transform our lowly bodies so that they will be like his glorious body."[119] We know this will happen because the God who speaks hope through his servants—from Abraham to Paul— is both *able* to keep his promises and *faithful* to keep his promises.

The seeds mentioned above? They will rise up and bloom into flowers, not small but bountiful. They will not be of earth tones, but brilliant, individually and beautifully sculpted, each one. Roses will open up with deep red petals of velvet. Dahlias will burst forth in clusters of pastels atop delicate stems of support. Daffodils will announce spring through trumpets of gold. Lily of the Valley will lace gardens of bold begonias. All will be changed. All will burst forth in glory.

And so we, too, will rise from death to glorious life in Christ. It will happen. We have God's Word.

So it will be with the resurrection of the dead. The body that is sown is perishable, it is raised imperishable; it is sown in dishonor, it is raised in glory; it is sown in weakness, it is raised in power; it is sown a natural body, it is raised a spiritual body.
(1 Corinthians 15:42–44)

---

[119]Philippians 3:20, 21

Swallowed up by Life

> *It was about this time that King Herod arrested some who belonged to the church, intending to persecute them. He had James, the brother of John, put to death with the sword.*
> *(Acts 12:1, 2)*

It hurts to lose the people we love—those with whom we've laughed and smiled, struggled and ached, celebrated and shared, mourned and wept, and lived and grown. We've walked life's paths together, and now . . . and now.

Imagine the friendship among James, his brother, John, and Peter. From the twelve disciples, these were the three who Jesus pulled aside to develop into the pillars of the church. Once fishermen, all of them, they'd dropped their nets immediately at the words, "Follow me!" They left it all behind, no questions asked. Together, these three went on to share exclusive front-row seats to some of the most awesome and compelling events in human history: the raising of Jairus' daughter, the transfiguration of the Christ, Jesus' explanation of the end times, and the agony of Gethsemane.

Certainly there were the "human" moments, the kind they would undoubtedly laugh about later. Like the time they were all standing there with Jesus, Moses, and Elijah, and Peter blurts out something about pitching three tents! ("Oh no, you didn't!") Or what about the time James' and John's "helicopter mom" asked the Messiah if her grown boys could sit on either side of Him in His kingdom? ("Oh, Mom!")

But now James lived among them no more, departed through a martyr's death. His friends and family would fondly remember old times, yet they could share them with James no longer. The love in which they cherished him, they now carried as a weight on their hearts for he was not there to receive it from them. Like Jesus at the tomb of Lazarus, surely they wept. For James was gone . . .

. . . from them.

But, oh, what awaited James on the other side of eternity! Like the repentant thief who suffered alongside the Christ, surely James was with him that day in Paradise. And as God proclaimed himself still to be the God of Abraham, Isaac, and Jacob long after they closed their eyes in final rest, certainly James awoke to join them in the land of the living. For what we mourn at the last exhale of those we love is celebrated in heaven as a first gasp of celestial air. As we watch our beloved hold onto faith even as their world grows dim, we know there ultimately awaits them a heavenly city where "the glory of God gives it light, and the [Son of God] is its lamp."[120] No wonder the psalmist marveled, "Precious in the sight of the Lord is the death of his saints."[121]

Death seems to us an inescapable force that wrests from us and consumes forever those we hold dear, but our God

---

[120]Revelation 21:23

[121] Psalm 116:15

who holds authority over all things proclaims quite the opposite! Like those who have gone before us, we who are in Christ will leave behind these temporary shells to which we have clung so tightly and, on that day, step into our heavenly dwelling. There we will experience in ourselves the glorious, eternal truth of the matter: What is mortal is swallowed up by life![122]

Yes, what is mortal is swallowed up by life! It is not death that claims our life; rather, it is life that consumes our death! It is unto life that we leave mortality behind! And though the fulfillment of this promise waits for us, we can rest in its certainty now and freely proclaim it through an eternity of new todays.

> *I know that my Redeemer lives, and that in the*
> *end he will stand upon the earth. And after*
> *my skin has been destroyed, yet in my flesh*
> *I will see God; I myself will see him with my*
> *own eyes—I, and not another. How my heart*
> *yearns within me! (Job 19:25–27)*

---

[122] 2 Corinthians 5:4

About the Author

Paul Nordman held several executive leadership positions in the property-casualty insurance industry before retiring from a thirty-five-year career. He serves on the advisory board of The Salvation Army Columbus Area Services and is an active volunteer in Kairos Prison Ministry International, Inc. His hope is that this book helps its readers to trust Christ Jesus in all things and to experience fullness of life in Him.

Paul and his wife, Peggy, live in Columbus, Ohio, as do their son, Matthew, daughter-in-law, Gwen, and granddaughter, Abigail. Paul can be found writing most mornings at an area bakery cafe, with a pen in one hand and a mug of coffee in the other.

CPSIA information can be obtained
at www.ICGtesting.com
Printed in the USA
FFHW02n2204120818
47730573-51394FF

9 781498 480642